They work to save our earth for free!
Let's help them!
Please think!

How to Save Our Earth!

Book #1 The Truth

by

Eric the Blue Sage!

DORRANCE PUBLISHING CO
EST. 1920
PITTSBURGH, PENNSYLVANIA 15238

Dorrance Publishing Co
585 Alpha Drive
Suite 103
Pittsburgh, PA 15238
Visit our website at *www.dorrancebookstore.com*

ISBN: 978-1-4809-2037-8
eISBN: 978-1-4809-2152-8

They work to save our Earth for free! Let's help them! Please think! For our grandkids!

If my soul was in control I would not be buried. I wouldn't be burned! I would be used to feed other living things, a nut tree, a bird, a worm. To live on in other living things The why it should be! <u>Eternal life</u>!

Think understand! It is fun. It is real! There are no games. Think, understand, and know! Think past your programming! I understand! Can you?

Eric the Blue Sage!

Enjoy the story. Read past <u>my mistakes</u>! Think! Are you programmed? Yes!

Eric the Blue Sage!
PO Box 1196
Fredonia, AZ 86022

P.S. It does not matter who says what. It is the thought that counts! Not the person, not the gift—the . <u>Not the grammar</u>! The thought! Think!

CHAPTER ONE

The captain came into Tony's cafe drunk! Tony opened at 7. It was 6:30A.M., he left the front open for regulars!

He was yelling, "Is anyone here?"

"Yes!" Tony said.

"Well, I'm Captain Jack! I demand service. Send me your best waitress now!"

Tony was small and slight, but he could see Big Rohn coming in the front doors! Rohn would take care of him! "Screw you!" Tony said. "I am the owner! It is my right to refuse service to anyone. You're it! Get out!"

"Oh yeah! Who's going to put me out?"

"Big Rohn!" Tony said looking at Big Rohn. The captain turned and looked at Big Rohn.

He said, "Okay!" He walked out!

At 10 a.m. the captain came back! He was not drunk. He had changed clothes, shaved, combed his hair, and changed his attitude! He told the waitress he would like to talk to Tony when he had time! Tony came out with two cups of coffee and sat down without saying a word! Well, Captain Jack did not deserve any slack, but Tony gave him some! He knew we all have hard times; this may be his!

The captain said, "I am sorry for earlier! I will not do that again! I am Captain Jack. I have sailed the seven seas and more! I want to talk to you when you have time."

"Now is okay. We are not busy!"

"Well," he said, "I have heard about the people of the trailer park! The ranch and you! I wanted to know if they are real! I have been on the ocean, drifting for weeks at a time with nothing to do but think, and I have thought. I think I understand! The Earth is dying and will die—if we 'the people' don't start trying to save her!"

"Yes!" Tony said.

"You know you are an understander! I don't run into many people that are! How many understanders do you have?"

"I would say about 6,000. Not many in the whole world!"

"But you are growing!"

"Yes! We are. We have grown a lot in the last few years!"

"Do you think it will go on?"

"Yes, knowing that we are right!"

"We have to fight to save Earth! That is what we are doing, right?"
"Yes!"

"How did you hear about us?"

"My granddaughter robbed a bank at 17-years-old. She had no good reason to do it! What is wrong with our youth?"

"Programming," Tony said.

"Yes!" Jack said. "One of her friends had told her dad about a place, a ranch for troubled girls. They got her out of the mess she was in and sent her to the ranch! It has been very good for her! She started writing to me again! I was thinking that I was the only one who understood! But when I got her letters telling me about the ranch and how nice it was, I started thinking maybe someone else does understand!"

Tony said, "We the people of the park, the cowboys, a lot of people are doing what we can to save our earth! We understand!"

"I am leaving tomorrow. I will take a ride through the trailer park this afternoon. I am leaving you a check for 20,000 dollars. I want you to show me what it did when I get back! I know the dollar is not what it was a few years ago, but it should be enough to do something!"

Tony asked the captain if he would like some food and said, "I have a few things I have to do in the back! It won't take long."

"Yes. Ham and eggs sounds good!"

The captain liked Tony! *He is a good man*, he thought! He wondered if he heard someone say rubber eggs. It reminded him of a cook he had on board ship once! He would boil eggs so long you could bounce them. They, he and Cookie, would talk about tides and having a place of their own! What was going on in the world? How they could change it? How they felt helpless, powerless, and useless. They decided to cut back on buying, using—fuel and anything they could! That had been about ten years ago! They never did come up with a plan to save the world! They were not like the people of the park! They had a plan. They were making their little part of the world better, bigger, greener! It was great, and now he knew someone was doing something! He wanted to be a part of it and with the check, he would be. He remembered the day Cookie left! He said he had found a small farm in a small town. He was going to see how green he could get his place to be. Well it's never too late to help!

Tony brought out his ham and eggs! Tony said, "Okay, make it out to The Church of Universal Understanding."

"Is that you?"

"No. It is us, the understanders!"

"We the people of the park?"

"No. It is we the understanders, the seers! We are growing! It is not just the P. of T.P. anymore! It is the girls, the ranchers, the cowboys, and the kids! We are understanding that it is US!"

"You know, Tony, I was thinking of killing myself two weeks ago! I could not think of anything to live for! Then I got a letter from my granddaughter that told me about going to the ranch—Archie and Nikki's ranch. It said she could not believe any place in the southwest could be like it was! So alive, so many plants and animals, so many birds! I came out to see it, but my drinking got in the way! So, next trip I will have time! I think I believe already that I will become one of you!"

Tony said, "You already are! I have a copy of the first part of Archie's and Nikki's book. You will like it! I will send it with you! How long before you will be back?"

"I'm not sure. About five weeks, I think. I am retiring. I have to finish training a man to take my place. He is learning fast! I want you to know I understand the tides! The higher the sea levels get, the bigger the tides, the bigger the tides, the more our earth will be out of balance! The more Earth is out of balance, the faster Earth will change! Not for the good! We the people have to change; nobody can fix it but US!"

Tony said, "Yes, I can see that! We the P. of T.P. are doing what we can to save her! You are helping us. I wish we could make it happen faster!"

Divide and conquer! That is what "They" are doing! Family, friends, etc. Teach them how to act! That is all we need! As long as "They" don't agree with each other, we will win! Think! Please! That's all I ask! Overload with information! Teach with misinformation! Program with shit! Then divide = CONTROL! The captain understands! Do you?

The next morning the captain picked up a hitchhiker! She was about 30 years old! She said she was lost in life, not on the highway, but she was lost! She did not know where to go or what to do! She said she could see that the people in control were not doing what they should be doing, to take care of our earth! She said she would like to do something to help save her!

Jack asked how she had come to understand this. "Well, I was working in a care center for older people. They were not that old, sick, or dying! They were sharp! Most of them were taking one pill with their swill! That's what Old Bill called the food! It was good food most of the time. Anyway, we had to watch them take their pill with the swill. Old Bill would hide his in his mouth, then drop the pill back in his swill and cover it up! I asked him why. He said it was a bad pill. It took away their will! He said his son had looked it up on the internet. He said that it made them easy to control! Mindless! Well me and Old Bill started showing the people how to hide their pill in their swill! It was great! The old folks started talking more and telling stories to us about what they had seen in their lives and what we were doing to our earth! How it was us who are causing the problems we are having! Floods, drought, wind, and tides—all us! We are the disease that killing our earth! They helped me see. To understand! We started talking about having a garden, helping to take care of ourselves and each other! They caught us hiding the pills in the swill! They sent me down the hill to the highway and told me not to come back! I started hitchhiking! I have told this story about 10 times. It's like nobody wants to hear about it or talk about it. It's like they are getting the same pill in their swill!"

Jack said, "I will tell you where to go and who to talk to. You will be able to help save our earth. You will not see the pill or the swill anymore! You will love it! He told her how the people of the park, the ranch, Tony, and the Church, would take her in and how much they were doing to save our earth! He talked until they got to the next bus stop! They had lunch! She got on the bus. Jack headed for the coast, thinking he would call Tony and let him know she was coming! He asked himself, *How many people were like Pam, lost, not knowing where to go or how to get there, but wanting to help save our earth! Worldwide? Millions? Maybe? How many are taking their pill in their swill, in their cake, in their water? How many are demanding the pill from their doctor, for themselves, their kids, their wife, their dad?* Jack decided he would sell what he owned and live in the park, or close by! He would do whatever he could to help the world see and understand what's happening! He hoped they were not too late!

Five weeks later, he came back to the cafe with an old truck full of his stuff and a briefcase full of money! He asked about a place to stay. Tony said Pam was in Bob's place and washing dishes in the back! She did not like being a waitress! He said he did not know of any empty trailers or homes!

Jack asked if it was alright to go in the back and talk to Pam. "Sure, but don't stop her from working. She is a little behind right now"

Jack went back and started helping Pam get caught up. He asked if he could stay with her until a place opened up that he could rent or buy! "Okay, but you cannot drink around me or in my house!"

"Okay. I have stopped drinking! I don't want it anymore. I've changed!"

"I get off as soon as all the dishes are done! I will go over with you and help you move in! I hope you don't have too much stuff because the house is pretty full!"

"Not too much! I have a recliner I want! Not much I can't live without!"

They went to the trailer when Pam got off! Most of his stuff was very nice. They took the old recliner and some of the other stuff out to the street with a sign that read, "free!" They talked for hours about his stuff, the park, the church, the ranch. She had not been there yet! She wanted to go out and he did too. They decided to go the next day she had it off.

He called Archie early the next morning to see if it was alright and to see if they needed anything! "Oatmeal! That's all. Tony had it," Archie said!

They left at about 9! Half way down the ranch road the truck died! Jack got out his phone to call for help! Pam asked if he had any tools. Jack said the old man who sold him the truck said almost anything you will need is under the seat! Pam removed the fuel filter and put in a new one. There were four under the seat! They were moving in 15 minutes! At the ranch, the house was warm, about 80°F inside and about 38°F outside! Nikki cooked eggs over slowly. They were getting more than they could eat, even in the winter! They had side pork and eggs. Jack ate four and said they were the best he had ever eaten.

"Why are they so good?"

"Well," Archie said, "The chickens are eating out of the yard and the compost pile. I think it is a good life for them, a good diet!"

They talked about the ranch, the church, the park, and the earth! They talked until after dark. Jack called and told Tony they were staying over and asked what time Pam had to be to work! He said 11 a.m. at the latest! They had rubber eggs, hash browns, and toast cooked on top of the stove, and frog legs, the last ones. On the way back, they talked about Archie's book and what the captain had told Nikki and Archie about the earth and how the tides were getting bigger, how he thought we the people are draining the water out of the land, and how Archie was right about how important it is to get the beavers back all over our earth!

Pam asked Jack, "Why aren't we the people talking about this on T.V., radio, our phones, our computers, to each other! What's wrong with us?"

"Well, maybe it is the pill in our swill like you said earlier! Or maybe most of us are so focused on making money, buying more, getting a faster car, a bigger cigar, a shooting star! Not being poor! It is how we are trained! To do whatever we have to to make it higher up the ladder! Who cares if we are cutting the trees, filling our seas, killing our bees, increasing the breeze, as long as I get my new toy! I have seen most of the lands bordering our seas. They are over-grazed, over-cleared—turning into dust! I understand, but most people don't want to hear that it is US! We are in control! People don't want to see, understand, or know what's really happening. It is my belief we are causing another Ice Age! I believe the ice ages of the past were caused by over-grazing. This time it is us, we the people, who are over-grazing our earth! Depressing shit! Ha! Let's talk about the good things that T.P. of T.P. are doing!"

"Tony, the church, bought a piece of ground and put a greenhouse on it with your money! They have fresh strawberries, lettuce, and a lot of things they did not have last winter! It's a good thing to have. The people of the park already had the plants in their homes and it's doing really well. I work over there at times, along with a lot of other people from the park. Tony buys or trades for a lot of the produce! It was amazing how fast they had gotten the greenhouse up and running! Tony knows about Monsanto as do most of T.P of T.P. The seeds from their plants will not grow, he, they, avoid them like a plague!"

"I know some things about them too! We had a chemist turned sailor on board ship! He had quit working for them. He went from $100,000 a year to the low 20s. He said he could see what they were doing. He said he could not do it anymore and left. We, me and him, stayed up all night once, talking about what they were doing to our crops, our food, our feedlot beef, and chickens. The one word I remember him saying over and over was 'cardboard!' He said he had tried to talk to people he worked with about it, but they could not or would not talk about it."

When they got back to the café, Pam could not believe how many dishes were stacked up. All Tony said was that it had been a busy morning! Pam found out they had had two tour busses at 9 a.m. with 96 hungry people! They, the people, tipped good and bought over 200 of the postcards!

Captain Jack took over, he could not help himself. He told Pam to start loading the dish washer with glasses and coffee cups. He had brought his own rubber spatula to clean the dishes with. He filled a sink with water to soak the dried egg dishes and silverware in. He started washing the pots and pans after the dishes were stacked and ready for the dishwasher!

At one o'clock they were caught up! They had lunch then after running two more loads through, they went to see the greenhouse! It was full of plants, old people, and kids. The kids were teaching the old people and the old people were teaching the kids. What a wonderful place, what a wonderful life! Why can't the world be like this? Think, Eric the Blue Sage!

CHAPTER TWO

Tony's Café
For the Cowboy and the Indian!

Rubber eggs! "Hey, did I order this shit? What did I say, and what did you say to the cook?" He took a bite. He was hungry! *This is good*, he said to himself! "Never mind," he said to the waitress. But she was in shock!

She said, "Over slow is what you said and that is what I said to the cook!" She was thinking to herself, *Nobody has ever complained. They all got good tips*!

Tony could tell—he could tell by looking at them how much food he needed to give them, how to cook it, and how to season it. It was like magic! Tony had not gone to cooking school. He had not gone to any school! He learned from watching his grandma and grandpa, and the customers! Some customers would say, "Whatever Tony wants to fix for me!" They knew Tony would give them a good meal, and a good deal!

When a new customer came in, Tony would come out and talk to them, if he had time! He would listen to know how you liked your food, your steak, whatever; how spicy, how cooked, how served! He wanted you to have it the way you liked it! He would come out of the back with a fork in his hand when you were eating and ask if he could have a bite.

He would ask how you liked it, how he could make it better! He wanted you to have the best you have ever eaten, and most of the time it was! Tony knew, he understood, how important a good meal was, how it could make you feel, and how it could help to heal. He knew a good meal could cure you, just as he knew a bad one could kill you!

Tony's grandpa was a witch doctor. His grandma was a waitress! She could see when something was wrong with a customer! She would talk to Tony. If needed, they would call the witch doctor! The cafe was the best in the world at curing people! All it took to cure cancer was talking and eating at the cafe! Most of the supplies for the cafe came from the trailer park or the subdivision next door. All the people had gardens indoors, and out! They grew a very large variety of herbs, vegetables, fruits, and nuts! People came from all over the world to live there! Most people were dying when they got there, most were cured when they left! They had talk sessions every night. They talked about how to fix the earth! They learned to understand that we the people are in control! We have to be if we are going to save the planet!

Tony would ask if he felt he did not understand something someone said! They would talk about anything and everything! The older people would tell stories about what they had seen in their lifetimes—how we were changing our earth! They talked about what it was like in the past, what their grandpa and grandma had told them, and what could be done to fix our planet. People would listen and ask questions when they needed to, but they waited until the person was done talking; they did not interrupt!

One of their favorite subjects was how much good the beavers could do! Their dams could control the flooding! How we could help them to come back? Their dams worked to water the mountains, to clean the water, to cool the earth! Mostly it was hard to understand why we, as a people were not talking about this! They could see after a little time listening that the beavers are a very important part of our earth, and if we want to save the planet, we need them back all over our earth! As soon as possible!

Tony was very understanding. He knew it was wrong to send organic stuff to the landfill! His garden behind the cafe was the biggest in town. He had a compost pile out back he was very proud of! That's where he grew his garlic and other plants that did well in the compost! He would talk a lot about how much his grandpa had shown him about raising plants. He talked about how bad bare ground was and how all the plants helped to slow the wind and hold the soil in place! The plants also cooled the earth. It was easy for him to see and to understand, not just memorize!

Tony's parents had died when he was young! He was in the back seat when they hit a horse on the highway one night! The horse came through the windshield! He had no memory of this! His grandparents had raised him in the cafe! He had learned to listen, to think, and to understand when he was young!

It was Friday about 2 P.M. when a new customer came in. It was rare, but Tony did not like him as he looked at him from the back of the café! He was not busy, so he came out to greet him. The customer said, "Are you Tony? I am Bob Smith, Bill's son! One of the stipulations in my dad's Will was that I had to eat dinner here for a week, seven days before I could do anything to change the trailer park! I am a lawyer. I have checked into it. If I want to keep the park, I have to do just that! I don't have a choice! What's the special?"

Tony said, "Well you don't have to wait, but we don't serve dinner until after 5 P.M."

Bob said, "That's fine. I will be back after five!" Then he turned and walked out of the café.

Tony could tell Bob was trouble! He made a couple of phone calls, then went to talk to his grandpa! He told him what was going on. Tony listened as his Grandpa spoke. "That's too bad Bill died. He was almost as old as me! I told him before he left he should stay here, but he wanted to see the world! He did see a lot of it. We had been talking on the phone once a week for years! He was seeing the world, but for the most part, it did not make him happy! He would tell me how bad the world is! How dry, how over grazed, how hot, how poor! Some of the time he sounded very depressed. He was trying to write to tell a story, but I think he gave up. He was in one of the oil countries when he called last. There was a war going on! Did his son say how he died?"

"No. We did not talk! How should I deal with him?"

Tony's grandpa said, "Let him talk. He will tell you what you need to do! Just get him talking. See what his plans are. Lawyers love to hear themselves talk!"

Tony called his wife to make sure she would be at the cafe when Bob showed up. He wanted to see what she thought of him! He called a few of the old timers, the leaders? No! They were sages, the ones who understood how great life was at the trailer park because of what they were doing! Why can't we change? Can't we understand it is us, church, schooling, job, TV, programming! Please think!

They, the people of the park, had been planting and growing for over 50 years! Tony was not sure, but he thought that Bill Smith was one of the leaders in planting and growing! He knew he was one of the men who would sneak across the highway at night and plant trees on the Army's ground! They never did get caught! Today there was a forest of the trees!

They were a great wind break for the trailer park! It was a healing thing to do! The men and women would plant seeds in their homes! Apple, apricot, peach, nuts, too many to list! They would take compost from their pile and water, dress in black, watch for cars on the highway! Not many after the interstate went in, then sneak across the highway! The old timers had put in many hard to see but easy to use gates in the fencing. A system was set up so as not to use the same gates too much!

The guards had become bird watchers. They were looking into the trees at the birds not at the fence! Some of the guards came into the café at times, one would ask about all the trees? Tony would tell them it was where the old town dump was, then change the subject! To food, birds, compost, anything! It was the old town dump before the base came in.

At 5 P.M. Bob the lawyer showed up. He looked like a new man! The suit was gone, he had a bird book, a note pad, a pair of binoculars around his neck, and a smile on his face! Tony liked this guy! And said so when he came out of the back to greet him! Bob started talking about birds, reading his list to Tony. He said, "House Finch, Western Tanager, Vermillion Flycatcher, Hooded Oriole, Hummingbirds, and Flycatchers." Tony interrupted to ask Bob what kind of steak he wanted. "Rib Eye," said Bob. Tony told Bob he had to get to work and he would talk to him after he cooked his steak. He told him to go sit with the girls by the window. They were bird watchers! He did!

The waitress brought him some coffee without asking. "Black right?" she said.

Bob thought, *How did she know?* He wondered what his steak would be like. Tony had not asked him how he wanted it cooked! He started talking to the three girls about birds, all of the girls were in their mid-eighties. All had cancer when they came here. None of them had it now!

The waitress brought out his steak it looked and smelled so good he stopped talking! Tony came out of the back with a fork in his hand and asked Bob if he could have a bite. Bob said "No! It is mine!" He put his arms around his plate and held his knife up!

Tony pulled up a chair and said "Please?"

Everybody laughed! Bob said, "Okay , but only a little one! How did you know how to cook it? It is perfect!" Tony said he did not know for sure but he could tell by looking at the customer! "Where did the beef come from?" Bob asked.

"Well, that's a good story. Do you have time?"

Bob replied, "Yes!"

So Tony began to tell him the story, "Well, there is a ranch north of here. About forty years ago the old man that owned the ranch died and his son from New York came here and took it over! The first thing he did was sell most of the herd! Then he put the beaver back on the creek! He keeps the herd small—about 10 percent of what the old man ran! He came by one day and asked me if I would like to try one of the loins off one of his beef, I said 'sure!' Then we went to the ranch to get it. What a beautiful place! So green, so cool, so nice! His wife and two young boys came out to greet us and we all walked out to see his beef and the beaver ponds. If you think we have a lot of birds here you should see his place! The cows were not spooky at all. You could almost pet them! They looked so shiny and healthy! He said they had grass and a little alfalfa from an old hay field. He did not grain them or give them chemicals. He killed them himself in the fall when the seed was on the grass, aged them, and cut them up! He was a butcher in New York. I asked him why he had taken most of the herd off the ranch. He said that he had read a book about how the West was when the white man first got here. It said it was a grass land with beaver dams all over the streams, ducks, doves, quail, rabbits, fish, with very little flooding and very mild weather! He told me he was raised on this ranch that it stank and he did not like it. He left and said he would not come back. His dad died and left the place to him. Him and his wife talked and decided they would see if they could turn back the pages of time! They were both glad they did! Theirs is a wonderful life. They home school their boys, some days they said they think they learn more from the boys! Then the boys learn from them! They had to put a chain link fence around the apple trees and over flows on some of their dams. But, all in all, they feel this is a wonderful life in a wonderful place!

Tony, by this time, had Bob's full attention! Tony continued; "That is where all my beef comes from! I won't buy feed lot beef! And with the crops from the trailer park, and the subdivision I buy very little! Most of the locals trade for what they need! We have a pig farmer there are three maybe four people with chickens, we all trade with each other! None of us are worried about making a profit! We think about eating right, keeping fit, and helping each other when it is needed! What we can do to make our spot on this earth a better place! How we can get other people to see and understand! That is us, we the people, are in control! I am sure that is why your dad wanted you to spend some time with us. What do you think of the place?"

Bob looked Tony in the eye and said, "Well! I cannot believe how I feel!

Overwhelmed! I came here with a plan to make money! The plan has changed! I want to keep the trailer park the way it is! I don't want to see it change! All I want now is to move out of L.A. and live here! I want to see my grandkids live here! I don't know if I can talk my wife into it. I don't know if she would be happy here, if she could be happy anywhere! I know I can be happy here! I have never seen a place like this! So many birds, so many healthy, happy old people! So few cars! I had a flat tire when I left here earlier. I was driving in the trailer park, some old man came out of his garage with an air compressor and a plug before I got the spare out of the trunk! He pulled the nail out of the tire, put some air in it, plugged it and had me ready to go in five minutes! He would not take any money. He said he didn't need it or want it! He was happy to help!

He did ask what I was doing here. I told him I was Bill Smith's son! Then he told me how my father took him under his arm and how he had changed his life. He said my father had saved his life! He had cancer when he got here, but with a good diet and a change of mind he beat it! He had planted over 100 trees in the forest south of town! How him and my father would meet at Tony's Cafe every night and talk! He said they would talk about changing our earth, what could be done to fix the problems! He said he would like to see what he had written. He gave me a copy of a few pages out of his book! Why I don't rake leaves, or pull weeds!"

Tony said, "Oh, that's Eric. That's all he talks about! How to improve the earth!"

Bob continued, "I pulled over on the side of the road and read what he had given me! I have never read anything that made me think so much! When I was reading a little bird flew across the hood of my car and lit in the yard next to my car! I did not know what kind of bird it was, so I got out my bird book and my binoculars. He acted like a little chicken! Scratching, kicking leaves all over the place and eating the bugs from whatever he turned over! He was a Green Tailed Towhee! That's when I started my list of birds! I have never seen so many birds in my life! What a great place to live, so peaceful! That's when I decided I did not want to change the trailer park!"

Tony said, "Well, I have to say. I was worried when I first met you! I am glad you came around!

"Tony?" Bob asked, "I know my grandkids would love it here! What are the schools like?"

"We don't have one!" Tony said, "The parents want to homeschool there kids! That means almost no taxes! We use 1/4 the power of L.A. per person. We have no sewage plant. We use all of our waste to feed the plants of our earth! We use very few chemicals! We like it like it is! We don't want change! We don't want a Walmart! We don't watch much T.V.! Most of us chose not to watch even when we can! We have had enough programming! We have seen enough of what's going on in our world to know if we're going to change what's going on. We have got to change at ground level? We are doing it right, are you? We the people of the park are thinking! Do I want my kids to go through what

I went through? Hell no! Memorization! Hell no! It is programing! Learn to think the way they want us to think? Bullshit! I want my kids to understand! Not memorize! They the parents want the kids to know they can do something to help save the earth!"

Bill understood. Tony understood. Now Bob understood! He had to call Bill's wife and ask if he could have Bill's writings. He knew he was trying to fix the earth! She called the next day and said they were in the mail! She said she knew he was on the right track, but she couldn't read them because it was too depressing! Tony had a hard time with Bill's writings until he hit this paragraph:

> *I know we have it right at the Trailer Park! Trade, reuse, fix anything you can, don't drive unless you have to, don't burn, buy, watch T. V.! Don't play their games unless you have to! Think what can I do to save the planet? What <u>can</u> <u>I</u> do to help? House plants? Tomatoes growing in the kitchen? <u>Can I</u> live with that! I can live with that! Think! We have to change if we want to go on living on our earth! Can you plant a tree, a bush, a flower, a weed! Anything organic is good on the surface of our earth! It holds in moisture, it helps slow the wind to cool our earth in the summer and warm it in the winter! The surface of earth is like a sponge! That's the way it should be, the more organic material on the surface the better off she will be! Tree leaves, grass clippings, horse shit, all of this is better left on the surface of the earth! Do your best to not send any organic stuff to the landfill! If only I was King of the World!*

Tony liked that paragraph! He read it that night at the cafe! Everybody liked it. They made a list of rules for the subjects:

1. Instant beheading for anyone killing a beaver!
2. All organic materials, man, cow, tree, lawn clipping, etc. must remain on the surface of the earth!
3. Everyone had to have a garden! Indoors, or out! From two years old and up!
4. Our, your waste, from your home had to go for fertilizer, or mulch, to feed the plants!

Old Jim, he did not interrupt! He must have something important to say! "You guys must be missing a few brain cells! We are God, King, and Controller of the World! We are it! What we do does make a difference! Think!"

You have to understand organic material stuff has to remain on the surface of the earth! If she, our earth, is going to survive, we the controllers, the gods, the doctors, the kings, the captains, the bosses, the lawyers, etc. We have to choose! We can take control from the ground up! It's the only way to go! I have been thinking about this for years! I understand it! Ask! I will talk if you will listen! Understanding is knowing! I know not from books, but from life! I have seen it. We are in control, like it or not! We the people, herd the grazers. We bury or burn our dead. The organic matter is not part of our earth's protective cover, the organic matter that cools her in the summer and warms her in the winter! Eternally, life is not dust or ashes. Eternal life is living on within other living things.

Years ago, when Tony was a kid, he had asked Jim where did the cows come from? Jim said, "We, the people, brought them here! We did not understand what we were doing! We imported them from all over the earth, all the cows, horses, sheep, goats we could! We the people along with the rest of the grazers have over grazed the South West, the earth! We put a lot more animals on the range than it could handle! It was a grass land and now most of it is dirt!' He was saying the same thing now!

Jim kept talking and I knew what he was talking about! I understand! We need to stop the flow of money, power, and control to the top! We the people can control from the ground up! But we have to understand to know we can! Jim was saying too many things are wrong with how we run our earth! We should not burn or bury any of our organic matter, it should be used for food, mulch, ground cover, building materials, and etc. To not use the reusable stuff is a sin! We should be reusing the brick, wood, and etc. Using a track hoe to tear down anything is wrong! We should be using man power! Man power can save the reusable stuff! Help! Save our earth! Think! That is like programming at work! Big money is in control!

We need to learn how to be traders, not buyers! Saving our earth is more important than the economy! Please think about what you can do to help! To recycle is to reuse, you should not be sending anything useable to scrap, the dump or landfill! If it can be saved, save it! It is the money people controlling us! Advertisement is killing our earth! Think! Programmed, we are.

Tony asked Bob if he could fight the State, and the U.S. Government? Without blinking an eye, Bob said, "Yes!" "That's what I have been doing for years! It will be easy to win any case, with pictures of this place and the park people testifying!"

"What's going on?"

Bob said, "Well, the State wants to put in a sewage plant, and the U.S. Government wants to put in a water treatment plant! We don't want either one! Things are good the way they are! The waste from our homes feed the forest on the other side of the highway. The water from the wells is wonderful the way it is! We don't want treatment chemicals added to our water! From what I understand the fluoride they use is bad. It shouldn't be added to our drinking water! There is a book called, *Cancer: Step Outside the Box*, by Ty Bollinger. It says fluoride added to the water will reduce a person's power to resist domination! We the people are passive enough without the help of the Government!

"The birds eat the bugs. The bugs aerate the soil. The aerated soil holds the moisture to feed and water the green! Don't rake the leaves. Plant more trees! Think! I am right! Please, think! We the people are in control if we want to be! It is us. The world is watching! What are you doing to save OUR earth? If the earth outside your home is green, cool, and moist the bugs will not come inside unless you leave food out for them! You are in control of saving our earth. What are you going to do?"

After a while Tony asked; "Would you like to go out to your dad's place? We could do it first thing in the morning. Will that work for you?"

Nodding in agreement Bob said, "Yes, first thing in the morning after breakfast, say 10:00 A.M.?"

"That's fine!"

"Okay. See you then. We can walk from here. Bring your bird book, binoculars, and list. You will need them!"

For breakfast, Bob had rubber eggs "over slow" with hash browns and coffee. Tony said he would talk to Bob about his diet later! Bob left a $10.00 tip for the waitress, and a handwritten apology for the first time he ate at the café!

They left the café walking! Sunshine, blue sky, birds singing, a great morning! Tony said, "I wish I could do this every morning!"

Bob asked, "Why can't you?"

Tony said, "Well, with the morning rush, I wind up talking about what was said the night before. I just don't have time! I think I will start telling them I am going for a walk and leave! If they want to talk, they will tag along!"

Bill's trailer was next to the highway, but you could not see it! It was over grown with so much green it was invisible! Tony opened the door; it was unlocked! The inside was neat and clean!

Bob asked, "Why?"

Tony told him that when Bill left, he had said, "If anyone needs to use this place, let them. If they can pay, send me the money. If not, it is okay—just let them use it!" Bill did not need the money. His income from the park was about $50,000.00 a month! Rent was whatever you could afford to pay, from $0 to $1000.00 a month! Some of the people left their trailer to Bill when they left! Some people left him everything they had when they died!

Bob said, "I know I have been doing his taxes for years! What a mess some years! He would send a shoe box full of papers! Most of the time I had to guess what half of them were, I know he over paid on his taxes! But he would not talk about them, he said he knew I could handle it, and changed the subject! Last year he gave one million dollars to a small village in Africa! All he said was that they need it!'

Bob asked about the humming bird feeder in the window. "Who filled it?"

Tony said, "It could be anyone. I'm sure he talked about it with someone before he left!"

"How long has he been gone?"

"I don't know for sure. Maybe five years?"

"Who runs the park?"

"The people. It's kind of like we the people of the park have control. I can find out if you want!"

"Well," Bob said, "I guess you have a set of your own laws written down that the people live by."

After thinking for a minute, Tony said, "Not that I know of! It is by the people of the park! They do whatever they have to do to make it right for the park, the people, our little piece of the earth! I have seen them vote in the café, maybe two times. Once was for our general store! It is like a bit of the old west. I will take you over there and show you one day! Mostly, it is an order and pick up point, people don't run to the big city unless they have to, they walk over to the store and have whatever it is picked up for them! Big items will be dropped off at their door and taken in for them if needed. They all work and talk together! They will wear out a lawn mower or tiller sharing it with the neighbors. They don't have their own most of the time! It's nice the way they share! They understand, if they don't keep control someone else will! They do not want some over-educated idiot running the park the way it is with our government and the world! They know this is a free country! We can do what we want! We will fight if needed! We all like to think, talk, listen, and understand! We will do what's right for our park! I think the park is destined to be a very important part of saving our earth! I think we, the people of the park, can help to save our earth! We have control!"

Bob asked if they could go to the store. He wanted to see it! Tony said. "I will take you, but then you will be on your own. I need to get back to work for lunch!"

Bob walked into the store. No one was there. He stared at the place. Bulletin boards where on every wall! *"Wanted: Someone to help me with upkeep." "Wanted: Someone to cut a path to my front door." "Wanted: Someone to help me with writing my book!"* Most were dated, but there were not many old ones! Then on the next board it said: *"Free lawn mower," "free car, free chair, free tools, free trailer, free truck!"* This was a big board! Unbelievable! Then there was one that said: *"Trade food for work! Will trade for anything!"* Bob was lost and overwhelmed! He would come back later. He went to the café to gather his thoughts. "Traders."

Tony's thoughts were interrupted by customers. It was Base Commander Archie, with a seeing-eye dog and a trainer! Bob came in and sat down by himself! Tony could tell he was lost in thought! Archie said, "This is Lucky, my new dog, and our trainer, Nikki. We want to talk to you about a few things! We received a letter a few days ago that said our government. . ."

Tony held up a finger and interrupted him. "Hold on a minute!" He called Bob over to listen in.

Archie continued, "The letter said they want to put in a water treatment plant at the base! I, well, we sent one back, telling them that our water is very good the way it is and we will fight to keep them from putting chemicals into our water!"

Tony looked surprised! He said, "Wow! I had no ideal. I kinda thought we were on different sides of the fence!"

Archie said, "What? You think because I am old and blind I cannot see? Tony, we have been seeing each other for 30 years or more. I know the town has been planting trees. I know the town runs their sewage to the great forest! I know the town is still planting trees! We who understand, love it! It is the best thing that can happen to our earth! Did you know we have the second greatest forest in the world on the South side of the base? I started it! We, the old timers, are helping to make the new guys understand, the way you do! We know we are doing the right thing—to plant, grow, to keep the organic stuff on the surface of the earth! Hell, we punish the men by not letting them work in the base garden! What do you think? Have we both understood for years?"

Tony replied, "Yes! I think we have, but we could not talk openly and honestly because of your job! How long have you been retired?"

"Two weeks, but I still go to work every day. I want to! I have no power, but I know I have control! I know! They all ask me questions! I know! The men ask me about the beaver on the lower end of the base! I ask them what they think about them. You should have heard their answers! Unbelievable! Why do we send our kids to school, if not to be programmed? To learn to think the way they—the money people— want! To learn to act the way they want! To learn to follow orders the way they want! To learn to chase the dollar the way they want! To learn to buy, burn, bury, dig, and kill our earth the way they want, to be a good boy! Don't fight! I will fight to save this part of the world—the park! What do you think, Tony?"

Tony said, "We will fight if need be! We just got a new lawyer, Bob Smith! He is Bill's son!" Bob and Archie shook hands. "He is on our side! When he got here he had other plans, but he came around fast after two hours in the park! He is a bird watcher!"

Archie said, "You know, that is what I miss—seeing the birds! But, Nikki and I have got a good thing going. She tells me what they look like and I tell her what they are, then I do their song to see if they answer. Most of the time they do. I have been practicing for years! I love it and Nikki is enjoying it too! Tony, is Nikki smiling?"

"Yes. She's grinning like she is in love with life! She is enjoying herself!" said Tony.

Archie continued, "She is part of my settlement from our government. I lost my sight from watching an atom bomb test! I don't like to talk about that. I haven't been able to see good for years! My doc says I have to have both the dog and Nikki for some time. I have other problems. I want to talk to your dad when he has time!"

Tony said, "I will let him know."

Archie asked, "Can we meet here at the café?"

Tony told him, "No! You two must be able to talk! The café has too many people!"

"Is there an empty trailer I can rent or buy?"

"I don't know. I will ask! My granddad comes by almost every morning about 10 A.M. Come back in tomorrow. By then I will know about the trailer!" Tony told him.

The next day when he came into the café, Tony told Archie he had a trailer in the park ready for him to move into. His granddad had agreed to meet Archie there! Tony's granddad added two things to Archie's diet, apple cider vinegar and H_2O_2, as Archie has more than one problem! Like he said! They let Nikki and Lucky listen in as long as they didn't interrupt! They talked about saving the earth, beavers, grazing, gardening, life, and almost anything except Archie's health! Most of his illnesses were stress, work, and worry! It wouldn't help much to talk about them! So they spent their time talking about fixing our earth! They had a great time!

Tony's grandpa got his name from an old Indian woman when he was young: Chowcatoots. He wouldn't tell what it means. People called him Toots. Archie said when he first got to the base, the government was talking about closing it down because the water table was so low and the water was so bad! Toots said it was the same way at the park! Archie said he thought the beavers were fixing it! Toots said he was right; the beavers hold the water in the higher country and their dams stop the sediment to seal the leaks through the cracks in the rocks. Ever since the rancher up North took over the ranch from his dad the water has gotten better! The water table has risen!

Archie said, "An inspector from the Army had come to the base one day and said we had to kill the beaver, blow their dams and cut down the trees! I told him he was an over-dedicated idiot and I would cut him down before I would let him cut the trees! He knew I could; I have friends in high places!" The two of them checked out a Jeep and spent a day on tour, looking at the base, the trailer park, and the North Ranch!

At the ranch they had lunch with the rancher and his family! I think that's when the inspector changed his mind! The youngest of the two boys explained how the beaver dams hold the water, clean it, and stop the floods from flushing all the good organic stuff down the river. He knew what he was talking about! The inspector was amazed that a boy understood better than he did! Archie drove on the way back. The inspector was thinking and understanding!

The inspector said in his report that the base was in great shape and I was doing a good job of improving it and the water! He also stated that I should be left alone to run the base the way I was and that the water was a lot better than it was in the past! Of course he had the tests done on the water to prove that the water was better! When he left he said he would be back to live here if he could! We were friends when he left!

"I get a letter from him once in a while. He is planning on coming back someday! He says we, the people of the park and the base, have changed his life for the best!"

Then Toots said they had a retired weather man at the park, who for the last 30 years, had been keeping a log of the weather and it was always exact! He said this is the only place on earth that he knew of where the weather was getting better! He had proof he said that we don't get as hot in the summer as we used to and we don't get as cold in the winter either! We get more rain fall! The wind speeds have been slowed. The humidity has gone up! He said this place saved his life!

"I saw him when he first got here. He was dying! The doctors, some of the best in the world, had given him six months to live! He had C.O.P.D., cancer, crthritis, depression—hell he was dying! I am not a doctor, but I told him what to do if he wanted to live! He went about twenty days without eating anything! He was overweight! He only lost ten pounds, but he reset his immune system! He started feeling better on the first day! He drank tea, juice, H_2O_2, apple cider vinegar, and our well water! I tried to get him to start eating after two weeks, but he said he wasn't ready! When he did start eating, he changed his diet completely! He stopped eating sugar, salt, white flour, fats, French fries and any kind of fast food! He ate nuts, dried fruit, and vegetables. Well, after thirty years here, he is still alive!"

Toots and I noticed that Nikki was taking notes. We asked her what she was doing and she said she had taken short hand in college, and the stuff we were talking about was too good to pass up!

"I hope you don't mind! I think I will write a book someday!"

Archie said, "I think that's a good idea! Hell, join the crowd! Everyone in the trailer park is writing something!"

Toots told her, "Let us know if you need anything. We will do all we can to help!" "Thanks!" she said.

Archie said, "I started one years ago but I had a hard time putting it together!"

"I would like to see your writings sometime, if you wouldn't mind."

He said, "I would like that, if you don't make fun of my spelling!"

They laughed! They knew between them that spelling was programming, they could, can, and would read past the mistakes. You can understand past the spelling mistakes if you want to! You can see what we as a people are doing to our earth! Think! We can save her! We the people of the United States can lead the way! The rest of the world is watching the U.S. We the People! What will you do?

Nikki said, "I think it's time for your medication Archie!"

He said, "Not today. I feel good enough I don't think I need it!"

She said, "Okay you're the boss! Let me know if you change your mind!"

Archie looked at Toots and told him, "I don't know how much your treatment is helping me, do you?"

Toots said, "Well I am learning H_2O_2 helps if you have anything wrong in your body, mostly lungs, cancer…oh hell. You know I don't know. It seems to help anything! It's the same with apple cider vinegar. It works! I use it. What can I say?"

Nikki asked Toots, "Are you experimenting on Archie?"

He said, "Yes, in a way I am! I am learning that it helps to use H_2O_2 to heal people! The same with apple cider vinegar! But, I am not a doctor! I see it work; I use it! I am helping a friend feel better, live longer, and understand his body! I like helping what can I say! And I know Archie is doing better in just two days. I just hope it keeps working! It will. I have seen enough over the years. I know they work! I only wish I would have known about it years ago I could have helped many people over the years!"

"How did you find out about them?" She asked.

"The people of the park!"

Toots said, "They, a lot of them, talked about using apple cider vinegar for all kinds of cures! The H_2O_2 was the same but only a few people knew about it! Someone gave me a book, *The One Minute Cure*. That's when I really started understanding! I got pneumonia. The H_2O_2 cured it! That's all I needed; I was a believer! I have been using it for everything! It works on everything asthma to yeast infections! It is a cure all! It adds oxygen to the body! Cancer does not do well in an oxygen rich environment! It dies! That's when the trailer park got really famous! That's when the park started growing. It's four times bigger than it was back then! We are adding on all the time!"

Nikki said, "I've heard you don't use heavy equipment is that true?"

"No!" He said, "But we use it very little. Most of the work is done by man power! There is a crew of men and women in the subdivision that do everything by hand! That's who we the people of the park call when we need help! They understand how we want things done! No power equipment unless they have to! They do use a backhoe! They have a cement mixer they use on some jobs, but mostly it is manual labor! The way we the people of the park want it!"

Bob asked if he could join in their talks. They told him, "Okay, but there is one rule: you cannot interrupt!" Bob did not want to interrupt! He wanted to listen, learn, and understand! He was at Archie's trailer one day when the weather man came by. They started talking about why and how much the weather had changed in the last 20 years! Tony was there too. He asked the weatherman how much it had changed!

Mack said, "The summer highs were two degrees cooler on the average! Winter lows were four degrees higher; rain was up 1/2-inch per year! Not real impressive unless you understand the whole world is just the opposite. We are the only place on earth that I know of that has improved over the last 10 years! Wind speed is where I am really impressed. It is down 10 miles per hour!"

Toots asked him, "What do you think caused the difference?"

Mack said, "I know trees slow down the wind, but I don't understand this much difference and change!"

Archie said, "Well I'm not sure, but about 15 years ago a big cattle ranch on the South side of the base went under! Without the cows, the ranges were coming back pretty fast! There's a lot more ground cover, flowers, grass—it looks greener to me and I can't see! Nikki tells me about it when we go for a ride, or on our walks, she says it's pretty out there! I know it never used to be pretty! Maybe the low ground cover helps slow the wind. I know we don't get the sand storms the way we used to!"

Tony said, "This year is the only year I remember not having to sweep the sand off my porch! It was always there other years!"

Mack said, "This year has been a good one! We have had one and a half inch more rain than average! The storms- have been good, slow; soaking rain, instead of gully washers, as you old timers like to say! Like a tall cow pissin' on a flat rock! We have not had that. The rain has had time to soak in to water the trees, to cool the breeze, to help the bees! The bee keeper came by the other day! He said the bees are doing really good! Most of the hives are clear full of honey! He said it's the best crop he has ever seen!"

Archie said, "Are we doing it?"

Nobody talked! Bob was thinking, *Well, they have planted a lot of trees, they slow the breeze!*

Tony was thinking, *The beavers are watering the hills, fiats, the mountains do look greener! Scents! We got them back!*

Archie spoke. "Taking 4,000 head of cattle off the range is approximately 160,000 pounds of organic matter not eaten off the range every day! That has to help!"

Tony said, "You know with the beaver back and the cows gone everything is getting better! Bob, can we buy the ranch south of town, and get the grazing rights?"

Archie said, "I checked into it with help from Nikki on the computer! We can, and we should, if we can come up with about ten million! Let's have a town meeting at the café! Let's see how much we can come up with!"

Bob said, "I'll bet we can do it! I know we can!"

Toots asked, "How far is it to the ranch? We should look at it before we buy!"

Nikki asked Archie if it was okay for her to tell them about the ranch. Archie looked at faces! He got a few smiles and nods, and then told her to go ahead!

She said, "It's about 20 miles of bad roads! Archie had me let air out of the tires of the Jeep! We took three spares and lots of water and food just in case! The trip was about two hours in. The ride was not too bad with the tire pressure low! When we got to the ranch it was flooded. The beavers had a dam on the river that turned the ranch yard pastures into a pond! We took an old high road—a cow trail—around the pond to the house. It had running water in the house a black plastic pipe with a steady stream running into the kitchen sink! The pack rats had moved into the house.. It was bad! It stinks. I would not want to try to clean it or to live in it! We saw deer, rabbits, and one lone old horse that came to see us at the ranch! There were lots of birds! The range did not have much grass on it, but there were a lot of other plants, flowers, weeds, and so on. There were a few sand dunes on the road, but not a lot. The ground had cover and not much bare dirt!" She stopped talking!

Tony said, "Let's buy it before some cow man can! I will call a meeting tonight! We don't want the cows back on the range! We want our little part of the earth to keep getting greener, milder, better, and bigger!"

THE RANCH!

Well it took three park meetings and two votes, but in the end, everybody voted to buy the ranch! We are a local government! In the first meeting everybody was against it. Well not all—but most were! In the second meeting Nikki got up and talked about the ranch, the ground cover, the beaver ponds, the wild life, birds, flowers, and so on. It was spring time; she and Archie had made a second trip to the ranch, it was beautiful! Flowers were everywhere. There was green, lots of birds, insects, animals, lizards, frogs, and snakes! They had to pick up and move behind the Jeep, seven desert tortoises. They saw mice, squirrels, rabbits, deer, antelope, and the old horse who had survived the winter! They gave him a carrot. He would be a friend for life!

On the third trip the house looked the same! There were pack rats. The water was running and the land was flooded—the pasture and corrals too! There was nothing but ducks, cat tails, muskrats, and bats!

They stayed overnight! There was no place to sleep but in the Jeep seats, but someone had modified the seats so they went all the way down! It was hard to stop watching the near full moon, listening to the night sounds of coyotes, whippoorwills, and the beavers working! It was hard to go to sleep! Coyotes singing in the spring! Every cowboy will go along with this! There ain't nothing like hearing the pups singing with Grandpa and hearing the stories they tell about how the West has changed since the two-legged rats have taken control!

Well let's think! We the whites have killed most of the beavers, and cut down most of the trees anywhere and everywhere we could! For the most part we are still doing this. Why? For who? So you can have a new car? To Hell with them! They are the money controllers! Let's change. Let's plant more and grow more! Let's do what we can to save our earth! Please think. Try to understand! We are the gods who are killing our earth! Whoa! If Archie could only have written that down, he might have a chance at selling his book!

"What are you thinking?" Nikki asked.

"Well," Archie said, "do you want to write it down?"

Nikki said, "No not tonight! This is the best night of my short life! I don't want to write! I want to watch, listen, see, understand, and think! Sorry!"

Archie smiled and said, "No, Nikki, you said just what I wanted to hear! You are seeing what it took me 60 years to see! I love it! Thank you for being here!"

Nikki said, "Thank you for being here, Archie. I love it! You, the ranch, life, lucky, can we live here?"

Archie said, "I know I cannot live here with the packrats. I can have volunteers from the Haz-Mat team come out and clean it up!"

Nikki looked at Archie with a gleam in her eye and said, "I have never felt so at peace and so alive or so at ease in my whole life! Let's bring a tent to live in when we come back! We—you—can have the men set it up!

Archie said, "No! We will plan our next trip after the haz-mat team has cleaned the house! We will think and talk about what we need to bring! I will buy a pickup truck, and trailer if needed! We will need a lot of stuff…unless you can rough it?"

Nikki said with certainty, "I can! I come from a small town in the South West. We did not have hot water unless we heated it on the stove. We had no TV and no phone. I went barefoot most of the year! It was a very different place! When I think about it, I think of what it would have been like without so many cows! Like this! My dad was money hungry! He had to buy a new truck every year! That's why I left! I could see he did not care about the land, the trees, or our life! All he cared about was money! More cows meant more money to him! I left on my 18th birthday I did not have much, a new pair of shoes that I got for my birthday! Ninety eight dollars and a thought in my mind that I could change our earth to make it a better place and a greener place! I told this to the army recruiting officer! He was an older man who knew you and your base! Sargent Sam?

"He told me all about the park and your base! We—mostly he—came up with a plan how to get me this job! Boot Camp! It was easy! Dog school was hard! The lieutenant, you know the type, was an over educated idiot, but Sargent Tea—that's his nickname—he knew about you, your eyes, and your base! He said the Army had been trying to get you to get someone to help you for over five years! He said you would not have it! You said your caretaker, old Jim, was all you needed! Well, they knew Jim was drinking himself to death! They knew your eyes were getting worse! They had a good plan by the time old Jim went in the hospital! They shipped me out that day with a rehearsed opening line, do you remember it?"

"Yes!" Archie said, "You said I have a choice. I can accept you and Lucky, or get out!"

I was not ready to get out. I like young women and dogs, so it was an easy choice to make! These have been some? Hell most of the best days of my life, since you and Lucky got here! Lucky is the best behaved dog I have ever seen! He listens when I talk to him and he understands almost everything! You are not as easy to control! But, I do things I know I shouldn't sometimes! You are good for me! After we get the house livable we can move in! I have plans for the pasture! I have an idea for the overflow on the beaver's dam. When we come back we will bring a big truck! We will bring furniture, culverts, head gates, clothes, and food, but hell, we will be living off of the land in two years! Think about what you have to have!

Nikki said, "Well, I can go without most everything in the summer, clothes, food, sex, but in the winter I need a few things like, clothes, food, and sex! I need a blankie, some kind of heat or a camp fire to sit around and listen to the night sounds and sights! I can't think of a better life!"

Archie said, "Whoa! I am in love! I haven't had sex since the 80's, but I'm turned on now! You had better slow down unless you want an old man puttin' the make on you!"

Nikki said, "Do you think you're up to it? If you are, go slow! Don't feel like you have to hurry! I like it that way! No wham-bam-thank-you-ma'am for me! If you are up to it, I don't care if we go weeks before we have sex. I like it slow! If I am in a hurry, I know how to take care of myself just like you!"

"Hey!" Archie said, "What do you mean like me?"

Nikki laughed and said, "What do you think I am deaf? I can hear you at night you do make noise!"

Archie said, "Yea I have heard you before too!"

"Really? When?" Nikki asked.

Archie said, "Well one night I heard you talking it was shortly after you got here! You were a little drunk, I had taken you to the officer's bar, and everyone bought drinks! You had me drive to see if I could drive at night! Hell, I have driven that road drunk, sober, lost in thought and asleep! I am quite sure I could drive it blind folded!

Nikki said, "You had at least three people wave at you that night Archie! You never saw any of them!"

Archie said, "I know I can't see good at night! Let's get back to the ranch. What will we need?"

Nikki asked, "Do you think the stove will work?"

Archie said, "Yes. We will bring new stove pipe, a chain saw, an ax, bedding, and food. There will be a big list! We will take our time and think about it!"

Nikki asked, "Archie, why do you think we are so open and honest out here tonight?"

Archie looked at her and said, "I don't really know, but I think it is what both of us want! No lies! I know we have not lied to each other yet, and I don't think we will! Let's go to sleep! We need to let the base know we are okay early, or they will send out a patrol looking for us!"

They were up before daylight and on the road! Nikki drove. As soon as they were out of the river bottom Archie called. They were already sending out the patrol! Archie told them not to and that he and Nikki were on their way back!

That night at the café, Nikki, and Archie told the people of the park what they had planned! To put over flows on the beaver dams with head gates to use to flood irrigate the pasture!

"We are going to plant fruit and nut trees, a garden, wind break trees on the South end of the pasture!"

Old Jim said he had a lot of starts they could have! Tony said he would like to see the ranch and he would bring tree starts and help plant them! Everybody started talking they, "The people of the Park," wanted to start planting now! Archie said he would let them know when the pasture was ready and he would love to have all the trees, and help he and Nikki could get!

The volunteers from the haz-mat team went out that week end along with other volunteers from the base and the park! They put in culverts to lower the water level of the beaver's pond! They put chain link fencing around the pond end of the pipe, so the beavers could not stop the flow. They put up new stove pipe. They cut fire wood! They moved furniture into the house Sunday and helped Nikki set up the house! They helped plan how and where to put the garden in and where to plant what trees. They stayed in the house and the bunk house the first night! The haz-mat team had made short work of the clean-up and started a compost pile with the packrat droppings! Archie and Nikki were overjoyed! Then everybody sat around a big camp fire. A few people had brought guitars, flutes, and squeeze boxes. They played and sang, each time they stopped the coyotes sang to them! A good time was had by all!

In two weeks the garden was in. They had over 100 trees planted, and the beavers had stopped trying to dam the chain link fence around the opening of the over flow pipe! The way Archie had it planned, with high water in the spring, the trees would be in the flood plane from the beaver dam. They were putting up a fence around the trees. The beaver had only eaten one tree! So far, they had been pretty lucky; the deer had not started eating the fruit trees! Most likely because of so many people! People from the base or the park were there every day and night!

The beaver's pond had a sandy beach at the North end—not a big one, but it had grass around it! People were swimming every day! The stream was deep in the middle of the pond! Nikki said the water was not bad. Archie said it was like ice. He would try it later in the year! After a few weeks, most of the work was done. The water had started warming nicely in the afternoons. Archie started swimming with Nikki! It was the best thing he had done for his health in years. He was already feeling better! He worked in the garden early. He sat in the shade in the afternoon and worked on his book with Nikki! She would tell him about the birds and what the beavers and the pups were doing! Nikki said one day that Archie's writings were good, bad, bitter, sad, hard to read, fun, funny, and right! She said she liked working on them, if he had time they would finish the book. If he didn't, she would finish it herself!

Archie said he was feeling good and he even thought his eyes were getting better. One day he was going to go to the base and have them checked! But not now! Archie asked Nikki, "Did I ever tell you about my idea for psychiatric help for people with a lot of problems?"

"No!" Nikki said.

"Well it goes like this," Archie told her, "The patient has a paintball gun with a limitless supply of paint balls, both him and the doc are wearing light clothes and safety goggles. The doc says make me out as who you want to shoot! Pretend I'm someone from your past! But, you have to tell me about it before you shoot! If you shoot me without telling me who and why, then I get the gun! If you lie to me, I get the gun! I want to help you if I can! If you shoot me, remember pay back is a bitch! What do you think?"

Nikki said, "I like it! It sounds like good therapy! Where did you get the idea?"

Archie told her, "We used paint ball guns on the base for training! Some of the men always got shot more than others! Mostly, it was the asshole who got shot the most! The ones that that shot an unarmed man or shot after the whistle! I guess that's where it comes from!

Archie had hauled in a lot of old filing cabinets from the base! In the fall Nikki found out why! It was because of food storage! Archie knew about Monsanto. He knew how to save the seeds for replanting! He knew mice would eat next year's seeds if they could. The filing cabinet and plastic bags would protect them from insects and mice! He knew how to save the earth! The problem was how to tell other people and how to get them to understand! It is us; we the people are in control! We have to stop! We must stop thinking the way they want us to think! More is better! Bullshit! Unless more is green! We are the machine that's killing our earth! We are the rats that are eating our planet! Please ask! I will tell. I understand!

Nikki wrote this down. She knew it would go into the book somewhere, sometime! Archie had lots of these. He called them think sheets! She loved 'em!

Archie went to see the base doc about his eyes! He said they were getting better, which was very unusual! He asked Archie what he had been doing. Archie told him about the Ranch, working, swimming, walking, and about the H_2O_2 and the apple cider vinegar!

The doc said he had read about both before, but he did not believe in them! He said he knew changing your mind was a sign of intelligence, so he would do more research. The doc gave Archie an old fly pole and a few lessons on how to use it! He said he would come down on the weekend and show him and Nikki how to catch fish. He had been fishing at the ranch for years! He said when Archie was leaving, "Remember ten o'clock, two o'clock!" Fly fishermen knew!

Archie drove slowly and made it back to the ranch at sundown! When he got there the can at the gate was gone! He drove in to talk to Nikki. He was a little worried. Nikki was sitting at the kitchen table! She had his M1 Garand and a bottle of his best whiskey! He gave her a long hug and asked what happened! Nikki was in shock! A little, not too bad! She said at about noon a truck with two men in it stopped at the gate and picked up the can! She along with everybody that come to the ranch knew not to pick up that can! The can had a binary explosive in it! She told him the man picked it up and shook it then threw it into the bed of the pickup truck! Nikki took the M1 out the back door of the house when the truck stopped in front, she went up the hill to the hide out. She sat down and started practicing her deep breathing, the way Archie had taught her! The men pulled over closer to the beaver pond! After a little while a rifle was pointed at a beaver swimming across the pond. Nikki could tell it was the mom. She had spent hours watching them work! She did not hesitate! She shot the can in the back of their truck! What a boom! She had put the rifle down and sat still peaking between the logs. The blast had blown out the back window of the cab. The men after a few minutes got out and looked at the truck, said something, then left! She had sat there for about an hour or more watching to make sure the men were not coming back, then she came to the house and mixed herself a stiff drink!

Archie said, "Good job!" He squeezed her hand and asked, "Are you alright?"

Nikki said, "Yes. I feel strangely good! I don't know how to explain it, maybe happy?"

Archie did not say anything for a while he went out to the truck and got two sandwiches! Tony had made for him and Nikki, then mixed himself a drink! He ate his sandwich and watched Nikki pick at hers! Then said, "Let's go out on the porch and watch it get dark! I am proud of you, and those men will never come back! This will give trespassers something to talk about! It will stop them from coming out here. Remind me to put out another can! It will help to teach the beavers to not trust strange vehicles too!"

Nikki asked, "What was in the can? Can you tell me?"

Archie said, "Yes. It was ammonium nitrate and aluminum! It is safe unless you shoot it with a high powered rifle, or use a detonator! We won't tell anyone about this. We will see if someone tells the story, and see how they will tell it!"

Well the next time they were at the café, everybody was talking about the explosion! It had been a hunting guide and a client who wanted to shoot a beaver! When they were at the ranch the client had talked himself out of shooting the beaver with the guide's help! The client was amazed at how pretty the ranch was and by how green, how many flowers, how cool it was by the beaver pond! How many birds and animals! He asked why? The guide told him, "No cows, and the beavers!" He decided not to shoot the beaver! He was looking through the scope at the beaver when the boom went off! He, the client, wanted to go back but would not without the owner's permission.

He wanted to fish and bird watch! He was a hunter and knew what the boom was! He had made his own and shot it before! He had seen the bullet hole in the side of the truck! He left his number with Tony and a note saying how very sorry he was. He said to tell Archie how he knew it was all his fault! He said, I am a bird watcher, fisherman, cameraman, environmentalist, tree hugger, and I want Archie to know that I am a writer too! I am trying to fix the world, our earth! Archie would call him before he went back to the ranch.

After Nikki listened to the people of the park for two hours, Nikki was a hero! Nobody there could have done what she had done! They asked Archie if he could have done it. He said, "No, not after climbing that hill and knowing what I was doing! Nikki knew what she was doing; I had taken her out and shown her what the M1 could do! She did good with it; she learned to hold her hand on the top of the bolt to stop the clip bell noise. She had learned to use the range finder, home-made, she had learned to shoot the M1 out to 1000 yards! I know I would not want to be in a gun battle with her!"

Riding back to the ranch, Nikki was very happy, riding high! That was until Archie told her he had invited the shootee back to the ranch! It was a bad thing to say! He did not know how much it hurt Nikki until after he said it! He had to pull rank to get her to listen! He said, "Shut up and listen, Private! I will tell you when you can talk! He the shootee is a good guy!" He told her the story about him. He said, "Okay now you can talk!"

Nikki said, "I am sorry. I should have known you would not put me in danger! Lucky or you, I should have listened instead of getting angry! Sorry! It's nice to know there is a spark in you! That's the first time I have really seen it! I know when you yell at me you are really not mad! This time you were. I think that is why I said it the way I did, to see the fire, to know it is there! I will do my best to never see it again! Okay?"

"Yes! I pride myself on control. I do not like to freak out! I would hot worry too much. Think about what you did! I have a lot. I am cool. I was cool in the war! Save the beaver! I am a hero!"

Nikki said, "I want to put this in your book!"

Archie said, "This is our book. Think about it! Can you drive? I want to write to help save our planet! Our earth!"

Archie said, "Yes. I will drive very slow and careful. I will like it. It will be good for my eyes! I will take over at the ranch road!" They talked as she took short hand. It was like a new language, she was always talking about the same things! She was making a new language to save our earth, with beavers and understanding! What we the people are really doing–killing our earth!

It is the blind leading the blind! The over educated idiots, the programmed rats, me, we, the people, are programmed! To chase the money, to want more, to buy more, kill the green on our earth and no one cares! We do have to take time to think! Turn it off! The T.V. the tape, disk, radio, computer, iPod, and so on. Think, why are we doing what we are doing unless it is to kill our earth! Why have more kids, people, or goats! Why should we want more, if it is us killing our earth? Why not slow down and think? It is fun to think and understand! Fewer grazers mean more green, fewer jobs mean more green! Unless the jobs are fixing our earth we don't need them, slow down, stop going, buying, and shopping.. Save our earth!

Do what you can to help, plant, grow, have a garden and a composted place. Even if the weeds take over, it is better than bare ground! She liked writing like this. It reminded her of Archie's think sheets! That's where it is coming from when I get to write like this! I am understanding our earth and what we need to do to save her! The people of the park understand! Archie understands. I am learning! Nikki, the bluest sage!

When they got back to the ranch the old horse was trying to eat the garden. They had chickens. They did not have chickens when they left, there was a raccoon on the chimney with one of their chickens! Archie was out of the pick-up in a flash! He had the gun in his hand telling Nikki to shoot him! She did! She had seen them before eating chickens, killing cats, and puppies!

They had a herd, a pack, a family come to their ranch. When she was about ten, she found one of the babies and brought it home! It was a good fun pet for about two years, then for no reason it clawed and bit the hell out of her in bed one night! Her dad killed it on the spot with a hammer he had in his hand when they ran into her room! She had learned how bad they really are from one of her school teachers after that! They eat the song birds and their eggs! She did not like them!

When she shot the coon it went off the back side of the roof! Archie went out back to put them in the compost pit! When he got close, the chicken ran away. When he got back out front Nikki was cleaning the M1 he asked why? It hadn't been that long. She said it did not sound right! He went into the house to have a drink and fix dinner!

They ate on the porch with the sun going down a nice breeze, birds singing, frogs croaking, crickets chirping , pups yelping, and the beavers working to save our earth! Let's help them! Please think!

The next morning when Archie woke up Nikki was in bed with him! She was sleeping hard. Archie laid there and listened to the sounds of the birds singing! A rooster was crowing. He had chickens when he was a kid. He didn't really like them, but he did like the eggs. He made plans in his head to move an old hen house to the head of the garden. To use the water from the kitchen sink to wash the chicken shit out of the hen house, and on to the garden. That's the part he did not like about chickens, cleaning the coop poop! He got up and went outside to look for eggs! He found two in the nest boxes under an old hen. It was too late in the year for chicks, so he took the eggs. Nikki was up when he went in the house she had a fire going, and the coffee on! She asked him where he had been. He showed her the eggs, and said, "Hunting!"

She told him, "I will like the eggs, but I will not clean the coop poop!"

Archie said, "You know me. I have a plan!"

"Okay!" She said and slid the cast iron frying pan over to the heat! "I will cook them, over slow!" It was the way a lot of people ordered their eggs at the café now! Rubber eggs, toast, hash browns, and bacon! Bob had started it! The waitress liked telling the story, ending it with the note and the ten dollar tip!

Archie used the truck to drag the hen house over to the spot where he wanted it! He put tin under the roosts on a good angle to wash the poop off! They talked about buying food for the chickens and decided not to! It was very seldom they got snow at the base, there should be even less here at the ranch!

Nikki said, "Fifteen hens and one rooster!"

Archie said, "I don't know how many eggs we will get in the winter, but it should be more than enough in the summer!"

Nikki asked, "How will we keep them? The eggs!"

"I have a plan," Archie told her. "We will use the water from the spring and make a cooler box."

Nikki said, "I will help, that's what we used on our ranch when I was growing up!" They built it that day. It stayed cool. It was not bad! Nikki asked about money, taxes, how they could pay that much?

Again, Archie told her, "I have a plan."

Nikki asked, "How? I know you have a plan for everything, but I would like to hear about this one!"

Archie said, "We will start a tax free organization, a church? Maybe? I know the people of the park will help if we ask them. Do you have any idea? What should we call it?"

Nikki said, "The Church of Universal Understanding!"

"I like it!" Archie said, "We will hang a box on the gate post for contributions! We will hold our meetings around the campfire on Friday and Saturday nights. We will talk about what we can do to save our earth! How we can improve our spot on the planet! How we can make the rest of our earth more like the base, the park, and the ranch!

"I know we have been taught to pull weeds, rake, and burn everything we can! I believe this is wrong!" It was Eric talking at the café, "All you have to do is look at the trailer park to know. How can we get other people all over the earth to see, to understand?" Nikki stood up; she started talking about the Church of Universal Understanding, telling them about what her and Archie wanted to do at the ranch. She said most of, over 99% of the people she knew at the park, and the base were already members! We the people of the park understand! It is us the people of the earth that are in control! The people in the café applauded lightly!

Tony said, "Let's start with picture postcards! We can send them out to everybody we know! We can share the story of the park, the base, and the ranch with them!"

Archie said it sounded good to him. He said, "Let's start with a picture of Eric standing in his yard grinning. It will be all green except for his face!"

Helen the lady that lived next to Eric said she had the picture she had taken it earlier, she passed it around! It was a very good picture! It looked like Eric had an Oriole setting on his head! He was grinning from ear to ear! Everything was green except for Eric and the bird!

Someone in the back of the café said, "Why I don't pull weeds or rake leaves?"

Nikki said, "That's perfect! Let's put that across the top of the card in red! What should we say on the back?"

A lot of hands went up! People started talking to each other. The voice from the back said, "It is us. If we want to save our earth, we have to do it! From the ground up, more green is the thing! We the people can change if we want to! The people of the park understand, do you want to change? Please think! A P.O. box number and address! For more information.

Tony asked who was talking! "It's me the shootee. My name is Dustin. I have been looking for this place my whole life! I want to be a part of you,r world if I can?"

Tony said, "You are! Do you have more thoughts on how to get the word out?"

Dustin said, "Yes! I have a lot of them. How about a weekly newsletter? How about books, a radio or television station. ?" Archie said,

"Let's start slow and go with the flow! We don't. Most of us don't want a full time job. We have been there and we have done that. They talked all day on Sunday! They planned the first official meeting of the Church for next Friday night! Rose, one of the bird watchers, said she had done the paper work for a church once before and she could help with it!

Archie said, "I want steak and rubber eggs for dinner. What do you want? I will tell Tony.

She said, "I will have the special, whatever it is!"

They ate and drove home tired! The rest of the week they talked and got ready for the meeting!

At noon Dustin showed up in the truck that Nikki had shot. It was full of chairs! Archie asked about the truck. Dustin said he had bought it from the guide. He did not want it anymore! "I had the window put in, but I am not going to have the bed fixed. I like it the way it is! That's the day I saw the light! The day I really understood! It is us; we are in control of what happens to our earth! It was before the boom that I understood! The boom was my wake up call, the day I decided that I am going to do something to help! When I got to the ranch the first time I couldn't believe how green, nice, and cool it was! I asked the guide about it. He said no cows and beavers are all it takes! I have been to the café every day this week. The people are going to have a pot luck dinner. I don't know but I think you will have over two hundred people show up! They are going to car pool so parking should not be a problem, but still two hundred people around a campfire is a lot!

Archie said, "Nikki and I have decided to have more than one fire! We will let T.P. of T.P. decide how many! We are going to visit and have a good time that is the only plan we have. Nikki came out of the house and asked what else she could do?

Archie said, "Nothing! Come over and talk to Dustin. He is like us, he understands! It is us, "We the people, controlling our earth! We have to accept the fact! We have to understand it is us! Before we can change it! Think! Who? Cut's the trees to increase the breezes? Who? Killed the beaver to poison the seas! Who? Spreads the disease that's killing our bees, trees, seas? US! Everyone all over the earth is watching us to see what we do to save our earth! What are you going to do to save the earth?

"Sorry, "Archie said, "It's like when I start talking about saving our earth I can't stop!"

Dustin said, "It's okay. I like to hear it! I have something for you and Nikki!" He handed Archie a fat envelope and said; "It's to pay for the mule deer I killed on your ranch. It was going to the guide, but he would not take it! He said he didn't want it! I don't want anything to do with this place anymore! I won't be back! Let me tell the story before you say no! We, the guide and I came in on the old mine road, south of here! The road is washed out about five miles from the river! We camped with the truck the first night. We started walking before daylight the next morning! It was perfect, the sun was coming up behind us, we could see for miles! The guide set up the spotting scope where we could see the river valley and the cliffs on the West side of the river! He said he could see four bucks, none as big as what I wanted! He said if I find him I will let you decide before we put the stock on him! He, my buck, was almost behind us when I saw the glint of an antler in the sun I poked the guide with my gun butt, and pointed to where he was. We watched his rack coming up the wash! He was big! The guide gave me his tri-pod. I got set up to shoot him when he came out of the wash! He didn't! The guide made a sound like a doe, the buck came to the top of the wash, picture perfect, broad side! One shot through the heart! I am having him mounted! He is a 38-inch wide a four point a score of 213-inch green, that's before his antlers dry! He is by far the biggest buck I have ever killed and worth every penny of the $5000.00 I gave to you. I have friends who would love to pay you five thousand for a land owner tag on your ranch! I think you could sell about ten a year, if you want! You would be in charge of it, unless you want me to take care of it!

Archie said, "Fifty thousand a year would help out a whole bunch! Do you really think we could do that?"

Dustin said, "Yes. We can write up a contract or an agreement. To make sure they do not kill a beaver or anything else we don't want them to shoot! We could give a reward to anyone who takes pictures of someone doing something they are not supposed to be doing. I talked to Bob the lawyer at the café the other night. He said we can fine them and take their guns, their truck, and everything they have with them, as long as we have them sign an agreement that states your rules! Any rule you want! It is your land. It is the T.P. of T.P.'s land! If you want, I will have Bob draw up an agreement, then we, you, Nikki, and the people of the park can make whatever changes we want to it! Archie asked Nikki. She said it sounded good to her!

Dustin said, "Here they come!" He was pointing up the road. "I will unload the chairs and park behind the house if that's okay? I don't want to be talking about the big boom all night so I will park the truck out of sight!"

Archie said, "Yes. Park wherever you want!" The people came in a steady stream, four hundred of them! They brought tables, chairs, food, drink, and some brought fire wood!

After they ate, Archie, Nikki, and Dustin went to the porch to watch and listen to the songs and music! "Nineteen fires!" Dustin said. After a minute people were going from fire to fire all night. Some were even dancing at times!

Nikki said, "I have never seen so many happy people at one time in my life!" Nikki and Archie told Dustin there was an empty bed in the house if he wanted.

Dustin said, "No! I like sleeping in my truck bed!"

Archie said, "If you have any problems, it's okay to wake us up just come in and start yelling at us!"

"Okay" Dustin said. "I am going out to the fires. I am sure it is close to storytelling time. I know there will be some good ones! Good night!"

The next morning Nikki woke Archie up at day light, "Come and see!" Is all she would say!

Archie asked, "Is that a moose?"

Nikki said, "Yes! I didn't know they came this far South! This is great!" Nikki went behind the house to wake up Dustin so he could see! He was up with a tri-pod and a camera! Taking pictures, changing cameras, lenses, and film!

"This is great!" he said. "The first moose I have ever seen!" They did not talk. She was watching him and the moose!

Nikki said, "Come in the house when you're ready. We'll have some coffee, cake, and rubber eggs!"

"Sounds great I will be there in a few minutes!"

Nikki was frying eggs when Dustin came in. He said, "Someone is coming into the ranch! It is early for someone to be getting here!"

Nikki said, "I hope nothing is wrong!" They were all standing on the porch!

Nikki said, "I think that is my dad!" As she ran to his truck! He stepped out and gave her a big hug! "Is Mom alright?" She asked.

"Yes. She is fine! I just wanted to see this place you talk about in your letters! Is that a moose?" He said pointing!

Nikki said, "Yes! This is the first we have seen of him but he is here!"

He said, "Your grandpa said there were moose when he first got here!"

"Dad, this is Archie and Dustin. You will like the stories you are going to hear!"

"Okay," he said, "but do you have coffee and some food? I have not eaten for hours!"

At breakfast the stories started. They ate and walked out to the beaver ponds, telling stories all the time. The moose was gone, but the beavers were working to save our earth! It was a great day! Dustin said at sundown he had to go back to work! He would be back as soon as possible! He left.

Nikki's dad stayed in the barn, or bunkhouse! He was on the porch when Archie came out the next morning!

He said, "This is beautiful!" Looking at the garden, the trees, and the beaver's pond! Can I run a few cows here?"

Archie said, "No way in hell! Not as long as I am alive! Or your daughter!"

"What are you guys? Tree huggers?"

Archie said, "Yes! I guess so! We want our earth to survive! We want to see more green! We want to save our earth! We think we have over-cleared, over-cut, and over-grazed for years! We want to see it, Our Earth better, greener! The more green we have on her surface, the slower the winds will blow! The cooler she will be in the summer. The warmer she will be in the winter, milder in the whole! The long run! You know what I am saying, don't you?"

"Yes." He said, "I have known for years, but I could not accept it! I sold three hundred of my cows this spring! I knew from past experience that it would be a bad year! I am going to follow Nikki's advice; I am going to cut the herd back! I am going to let the beavers come back on the North Fork! She has always been a very smart girl! I knew she was right when she was little, but like I said, I could not accept it!"

Archie told him, "You can be very proud of your girl!" He told him about the beaver war, the meeting, and the plan!

"Alright!" Nikki said, "It's time to eat!"

"Have you been listening?" Archie asked.

She said, "Yes, and taking short hand! Eggs are over slow. The hash browns crispy the way dad like's 'em. Bacon crisp the way you both like it. I think it would be a good idea to tell Dustin's story Archie, what do you think?"

Archie said, "Okay!" He started with the hunt and the money. Nikki's dad, Miron liked it. He kept asking questions. He wanted more details! They were out on the porch drinking coffee when the moose came back! He came over to see them. He checked out the garden, the fences, and the chicken coop! He even checked out Miron's truck! "A two-year-old." Archie said he had heard about them! "Fearless like us when we were young!"

"Fire!" Nikki said pointing. "Get the phones! I will get the truck!" All three of them were in the truck. Archie was driving! He made it to the perfect spot to get a phone call out in record time! Nikki was already talking!

"They say it is under control!"

"Bullshit!" Archie said, "Give me that phone!" She did. Archie said, "Who is in charge? I want to talk to him!"

The man said, "That's Shoots! Randy Shoots! He is with the Bureau of Land Management!"

Archie said under his breath, "Whitehorse Shoots! One of the best Marksmen the Army ever had! Tell him it's Colonel Archie!" he said.

"Okay I will patch you through!"

"Hello. Whitehorse Shoots?"

"Yes! Archie, how are you?"

"I am fine! I want to talk to you about the fire!"

"It's under control! Don't worry!" Shoots assured him.

Archie said firmly, "Bullshit! The wind will pick up in a couple of hours and it will be at our ranch at noon!"

"Archie, I have been doing this for thirty years! I know what I am doing!" Archie said "Randy there is something you don't know! This ranch has not had cows on it for sixteen years. The ground cover is thick and dry! All I ask is you look on google to see that you can stop the fire at the river! We have beaver ponds for water for the copters, and a green belt! A place to stop the fire at the river! Think! Bye!"

Nikki asked, "Is that all you are going to do?"

Archie said, "Yes. Whitehorse is a good man and a smart one! He will stop the fire! At noon the copters were scooping water out of the ponds fast, and at one o-clock the fire was out! Nikki, Archie, and Miron had been in the truck for the last two hours just in case! Watching! Talking, thinking! What is just? Who can you trust? T.P. of T.P. Yes!

They went back inside. Miron's phone rang. It was Whitehorse. He asked for Archie. All he said was "Thanks for the heads up! Bye!" Archie gave Miron's phone back and asked why he had reception?

Miron told him, "It's a satellite phone, my wife made me get it! But now I have it. I can't live without it! It works almost anywhere!"

Archie asked, "What's for dinner?"

Nikki said, "I don't know!" Miron asked if they had any cans.

Archie told him, "Yes, Nikki said we have beans, beef stew, corn, peas, green beans, and cranberries!"

Miron said, "Save the cranberries for another day, dump the rest in a pot and cook it. I will eat it!" It was a good dinner! After dinner they sat out on the porch and drank whiskey. They talked until after midnight! They asked Miron to come in the house to sleep. He said no he had a dream about his first horse in the barn last night that was real! He said he wanted to see if his nightmare would come back to see him.

The next morning Archie was up early. Miron was loading his bed roll in the truck when Archie got to the barn Miron said, "Well, my nightmare came back! It was dark as hell. She was standing right on top of me, smelling me. She scared the shit out of me! She was real. I moved slow, reached up and touched her on the nose! She turned and walked out of the barn!"

Archie said, "Yes. We do have an old horse on the ranch! I want you to stop by the café on your way home. Tell Tony who you are and what your plans are! He will tell you who to talk to to get all the trees you need to get started!"

Miron said he would have breakfast at the café! "Tell Nikki I love her. I hate to say goodbyes! I want to drive and think! Bye now!" He got in his truck and left!

Archie went for a short walk before he went in the house, then told Nikki what her dad had said, she said; "He has always been like that! It's okay. I am glad he is selling some of his cows!! He is one of us now!" "Yes, I think so too!! An understander! Hey I forgot, I put up a donation box on the gate. Will you watch the eggs while I go check it?"

"Yes. Take a sack with you. I walked out to check it after your dad left. It is full!"

Nikki came back with a plastic bag full of money! They ate breakfast then dumped the money on the table! "Almost $4000.00! What are we going to do with it?"

"I think we will have to put it in a bank for a church fund! We will decide what to do with it later! I don't want to have the meetings here at the ranch anymore!"

"Why?"

"Well, before the meeting we had a nice grass flat between here and the gate, now we have a dust bowl!"

Miron loved Archie and Nikki's ranch! He hated his own. It was kind of a dust bowl! It had had too many cows, horses, sheep, and goats on the land for years! He had known it was getting dryer, less grass, more wind for years. He told himself all it needed was more rain, but when the ranch got it, all it did was flood the river and wash the top soil away!

"It was time for a change!" Archie said,"Fifteen years without cows-grazers, and Archie, Nikki's, the T.P of the T.P.'s ranch was beautiful! I hope I can get mine to come back that fast. If I can, then I can live to see it turn green!

He stopped at the café at about 10 in the morning. It was almost empty! Tony came out of the back and introduced himself. Miron told tony who he was and what he had been thinking! Tony asked him what he wanted for breakfast. Miron said he wanted rubber eggs, crispy hash browns, and crispy bacon!

Tony left. He called Toots and old Jim. He asked Jim to call and find some tree starts. He needed 20 or more—enough to fill the bed of a pick up! He told his grandpa, "There is something wrong with this guy's health. I want you to look at him!" When Toots got there he walked up to Miron and said; "I want you to start eating oatmeal and beans! I want you to start drinking H_2O_2 and apple cider vinegar! How long ago did you stop drinking?"

"About two years ago! I still have a drink once in a while!"

"Once in a while won't kill you, but if you drink a lot it will kill you! Your liver is bad! I will write down how to use this stuff! Make sure you use it every day! Call if you need advice or help! He wrote down a couple of things for Miron and left!

Tony was back, Miron said, "Who was that?"

Tony said; "I think he is writing a book. I see very little of him lately! That's my granddad. He is a witch doctor! He cures cancer, diabetes, ADD and so many other ailments. I can't believe it! I called him for you. I could see there was something wrong with you, but I have no idea what! Toots can look at you and know!"

"He could see I had a bad liver. My doctor said if I didn't stop drinking, I would be dead in a year! Maybe six months! He did not say or do much, but I am going to do what he says! He knows!"

"Yes, I know that. That's why I called him over! They have your truck loaded whenever you're ready!

"What the hell do you mean?" As he turned to look. He said "What's this?"

Tony told him, "You are one of us now! T.P. of T.P. and we take care of each other! We do whatever we can to make our earth a better place to live! We have learned here at the park we can make a difference. We have cooled our part of the earth in the summer. We have decreased the winds. We have increased the rain fall. We have made it warmer in the winter! We understand and now you do to! The trees will have notes on them (the painted side goes to the South) as to where and when to plant them, and what they are! If you have any questions call the number on the notes it is best to call that number! Do not use chemicals on them! Let the birds take care of the bugs! You will lose trees, we have replacements! You will too! This is wonderful to know we are expanding! T.P. of T.P."

"How long have you been doing this?"

"I don't really know. I don't know how, when, or why it really started! It may have been my grandpa! Toots has been here about sixty years! They started the park and the café! He may tell in his book! He has never been much of a story teller or a talker! He listens better than anybody I know!"

"Well, you can believe me. When I say I will do my best! I want my ranch to look like T.P. of T.P.'s! I have a lot to do! I would like to stay and ask questions all day, but I had better hit the road! Bye now!"

"Have a good life!" Tony said.

Well it was back to driving and thinking for Miron! He had friends. He could talk, but he knew he should not push it! He had to go slow most of his friends were in the same boat he was! High gas cost to haul water, dry range, no end in sight! What should they do? It was time for a change! T.P. of the park know! They can and will help! But how to introduce it? Think! I am are you? Thinking? Take 'em to church? Hell no! Invite them to a party? Hell yes! He decided then and there! He is on the road. It is a constant variable! Right our earth! If we want to survive!

That is our goal! T.P. of T.P., to make it greener, nicer, milder, better for our grandkids! Think! That is the goal! So, what if you don't have grandkids? You know the earth will be better because you did not have so many! Think! That's all I ask, Miron the Black Sage! It is me I have done it! From the ground up! That's how it happens! We have to change if you want your grandkids to survive! We have to make the earth greener. We the people have to talk, to think, to understand! Think! If we can learn to understand, we can control!

Miron started thinking about having a party at his ranch, he could invite the other ranchers and the cowboys! He did not like public speaking, but around a camp fire with his friends it would be alright! He called some of the key people to get the word out! It would happen at four in the afternoon Saturday at the North gate! It will be a pot luck! All he was going to do is tell them what his plans are, to become a tree hugger! Ha! It would be hard and fun! After he told them he would listen to how they were doing on the ranches! How, or what they could do to make it better! He would tell them about the park, the base, and the ranch! If he could get them to listen! He would tell them about the moose, the beaver war! The plans of the T.P. of T.P. He would? He hoped to tell them how to save the earth!

He had let them know to bring whatever they needed, chairs, tables, etc. He would bring a cow! To roast! He killed a heifer that had a bad attitude, she was mean! Bitch was her nickname! He killed her himself and had his men help and watch, he was a packing, house worker, killing cows for nine years! He had done it before, the cowboys liked it! He hung her in the barn with a wet sheet on her to keep the flies off and to keep her cool!

Saturday he thought about calling Nikki and Archie! He would do better at talking and explaining! He called early, Archie had a phone that worked at the ranch now, Nikki answered! Archie had gone for a walk. She said she thought they would be there, she would call if they would not make it!

Four p.m. Saturday a line of pickups came to the North gate! Miron had been cooking a four hundred fifty pound beef! Nine ranchers, that's all! He had got up at four a.m. him and three hands had built a huge cedar fire, set up the cooking spit and started shoveling cooking embers as soon as they could with special long handle shovels he had made! Shit! Why no ranch hands? He asked "Why no ranch hands?" "We heard you had turned into a tree hugger, we don't want 'em to be around you!" big Rown said. At 6' 5" he was a Big Rown! He did not know how to take any shit of off anybody! Well it was not a very fun party for the first three hours, then, Miron got a call from Archie, he said he had ran out of gas about ten miles from the North gate! "I think it is my fault. I am used to the men at the base taking care of me! Wait a minute there is a line of trucks coming up the road! Don't worry about sending someone down, we will get gas or a ride!"

Well about an hour later Archie showed up at the gate with his new recruits! He had won over forty men, cowboys within twenty minutes! What the hell did he say? But Nikki was there taking her short hand! She read around the campfire! We all had different moms, dads, friends, churches, schools, but I will tell you, what you believe in, is what is true, we will do what we think is right! I, we, understand, trees, grass, ground cover! Slows the wind, cools the breeze, and causes rain on our trees, stops the diseases that are killing our seas!

Is it us, the U.S.? Yes! The U.S.! We are leading the way! We are the main cause of decay! That is causing our earth to die! To fade away! Please think! We need to slow down and think! Why not get the beavers back on our streams? Why not work to save our earth? Why not do what we can do to save our earth? Programming? Let's do it for our grandkids! That was all she had! She said she was not ready to see the three men who came up to help! She had known very few in boot camp and dog school! But it was Bert, Kent, and Jim! Her friends! She had stopped taking notes!

The men at the campfire started talking about our earth! What their dad's said! What they knew from riding the range! They broke up into smaller groups and kept talking and eating, they ate over half of the beef! It was good! Miron and Archie were by the beef talking! Archie said; "Well you did it!" Miron said; "No you did it!" Nikki said; "OK we did it! T.P. of T.P. are spreading this is good!" They, the ranchers knew it was a losing battle, they know it is harder every year! They know they have to haul more water every year! They know the cost is up and the profits are down! They know they can make more money on one deer than ten cows! Why not cut the herd size? They were all talking along the same lines, the ranchers and the cowboys had had time to think! Riding the range, the fence lines! It was easy for them to see, to understand! Do you know because of the way you were taught, programmed, or do you understand? Think! Please!

Archie was talking about what he and Nikki had planned for the Church of. Universal Understanding! It would be open to all, any that wanted to come! Anybody who wanted could get up and say anything they wanted! Big Rown said; "I was ready to fight when I got here, I still am! But I want to fight for our earth now! I own the old Jones place now! The big old barn is still standing, you can use it for the meeting house if you want! I will have my hands mend the fence, and the barn so we can keep the cows out, and the barn will not fall down on us! It is close to center a great place to meet!

Jim, Nikki's friend asked if the old boiler from the sawmill would still work? Miron said: "It was working fine when the loggers left. But how would we move it? You are thinking of using it for heat this winter right?" "I know my dad told me it was moved up there in two pieces!" Someone said. Big Rown said; "I have a low boy trailer, me and my boys will move it, it will be a fun family project to move it!" Archie asked; "Does the old Jones place still have water so we can start planting trees?" "Yes, but it would take some work to get it flowing!" Archie said; "Why can't we use the beavers to help the way they did at my place?" Miron asked, "How much do they charge?" Archie said, he had not received a bill yet but whatever it was he knew it would be worth it! The church had money if one of the understanders needed help with supplies for work, or anything else! Everyone was grinning, thinking about the bill from the beavers! How much would they charge to help save our earth!

It was after midnight, three trucks headed down the canyon, they had chores that had to be done in the morning! Most of the men had brought booze with them, but there had been very little drinking! Most of the beef was gone! Archie and Nikki said there goodnights! Lucky was still up, making the rounds from cowboy to cowboy around the fire getting talked to, and loved by the men! His belly was big, he was very happy!

Their bed in the back of the truck was nice! It was cold, but not bad! Nikki said she could not believe how good the party had been, how easy it had been to get the men understanding what they were doing! All it took was getting them started talking!

The next morning the coffee was on before Nikki and Arch got up! They had over four dozen eggs! They had been getting a lot more than they could eat! He got out his cast iron skillet and Nikki came back from one of the fires with fresh side pork! The coals from the beef cooking fire were still hot, Archie started cooking! The cowboys were cutting pieces off of the beef with their pocket knives and giving him a piece once in a while, the side pork, and cowboy toast! Coffee boiled! What butter? Who needs it? Eat what you got!

He would drive slowly. Archie would drive on the dirt and Nikki would drive on the oil! They would stop at Tony's to give them the good news, then on to the ranch! When they hit the ranch road, Nikki got her writing stuff out. Archie knew from his own writings not to talk! He got in the driver's seat. Nikki got in and started writing! After a while she said, "A little faster! I don't want you going to sleep! We want to get there as fast as you can without you killing both of us!

"Cool!" He said, "This is better than recess when I was young in grade school! He gave the truck some gas! He needed to get a feel for how the truck drove and how she could handle the road. He could see pretty good with his new sunglasses! He knew how to spot the rocks because of their shadows! He had been driving the road long enough to know where the bad spots were! Before long Nikki was laughing! Archie asked, "What's going on?"

Nikki said, "This is the same way my dad drove when I was little, but he could see! You can slow down a little bit. I don't want a wreck!" He did. Around the next turn the old horse was standing there with a girl petting him! Boy, was he glad he had slowed down!

The girl said, "We heard about this place and wanted to see it! I hope you don't mind!"

Archie said, "I have a few rules. How many of you are there?"

She said, "Two vans with seventeen people! We came on a one-day trip! Four hours out and four hours back! We can't stay long!"

When the two vans got to the ranch, Archie called them to come over to the house. He stayed on the porch He said, "First, this is a ranch road. You never know when some old drunk, mad, blind guy, will be driving too fast on it! Or worse yet, a kid! Get off the road if you can when you stop! Stay out of the road on the blind turns. Do not roll rocks onto the road unless you can roll them back off! If you see a dust cloud from a truck, you know he is coming fast! Get out of his way. His wife may be having a baby!

"Now, how many of you know something about edible plants out here?" Archie asked.

"Most of us know of some!"

Archie said, "Good. We can learn! Let's go over here for a minute! We can learn from each other!" He stopped and picked a pinch off some little green plants. Then brushed the sand off their roots and ate them!

One of the girls asked, "What was that?"

Another girl said, "Tumbleweeds, but I did not know you could eat them!"

Archie said. "That's what I wanted. We can learn from each other! I have a bunk house. Bring your own sleeping bags and camping supplies. Bring a heat source if you need one! No generators please! There is a compost pile over there. Anything organic should go there! Please be respectful. No guns! No fishing unless you take Nikki or I with you. Fire is very dangerous in this county, so ask before you have one! You are welcome anytime as long as you are caring! We are becoming the Church of Universal Understanding! There is a donations box on the gatepost for those who can! If you want to save our earth, you can come join at any time! We are growing! Welcome! We are the Understanders! Please think! It is us, the U.S. that is in control! The world is watching! What are you going to do?"

Nikki said, "If you want I will walk over to the beaver pond with you!"

They did. The two-year-old came out with a cow! The students came out too.

"What's that?" one said.

"A moose!" said another.

The last one said, "They have not been here for over one hundred years! What's going on?" Well, when they got back to the house, most of the students understood! The rest would understand before they got home! Talking, understanding, what a wonderful thing!

Archie said, "Dinner is rubber legs and frog eggs!"

Nikki said, He meant, rubber eggs and frog legs! He is a very intelligent man, but he has a warped sense of humor! One of his best jokes is what the frog said! 'Boy how time's fun when you're having flies!'"

One of the girls asked, "Where did you get all the frog legs?"

Archie said, "Nikki found out the frogs went into the muskrat holes to hide in the day time! We had a good time catching them! We had too many so we tried eating one. We liked them, so we put the legs in plastic bags so we could eat them later! We had too many. It's a good thing you girls came along to help us eat them!" The students had made a salad from what they had picked on their trip! They said it was the only place on earth that you could find all the ingredients; on the ranch! It had cattail shoots, wild raspberries, water crest, and pine nuts. There were all kinds of edible plants that Archie and Nikki had never heard of before! It was very good! Archie said they could come back anytime! Just bring more of the salad! It was after 10 P.M. when they left.

The next morning the pasture was flooded! The trees were watered! When Nikki checked the box at the gate there was a check for fifty thousand dollars! It had to be a joke! Nikki handed the check to Archie and said, "We're rich! Here is the note that was with it! It says, 'You are doing the right thing! More later, thanks! The Understander!'" There was no name on the check or the note! There was only a P.O. box number and an address. That was all!

Monday they took the check to the bank! "It is good!" The teller told them. Archi called Bob in L.A. to ask him what to do. Bob said, "Hold the check, don't put it in the bank until we get your tax exemption! I will start your paper work today! The Church of Universal Understanding, right?"

Archie said, "Yes, that's it. Let me know if I can help!"

Bob told him, "If it was me, I would send a note to the address telling them what's going on, and let them know you are going to hold the check until you get your tax exemption!"

Archie said, "Thanks!"

Archie, and Nikki, sent the letter saying, "Please come to see us anytime. You are welcome at the ranch anytime! Enclosed is our cell number, address, and a map, along with mine and Nikki's P.O. box numbers."

Well, Archie got a call the next week end! The man said, "My name is Matt, I had a cattle ranch forty years ago. Now I have an oil field!

When I got rid of my cows, I could see. I watched my ranch turn green! I saw the beaver come back. I saw the fish come back in the streams! I still like to fish with the help of my granddaughter! You met her when all my girls came to your ranch! They are good girls now. They were troubled teens! I have a school for them at my ranch. My wife started it when my granddaughter and her friends stole a car, got drunk, and wrecked the car! It was like a prison camp for the girls to start with! Then my wife hired a woman who knew how to talk to the girls! She was an ex-con! It has been a wonderful thing the school. The girls are running my ranch! They have changed the place! They have planted trees and reintroduced a lot of native plants!"

My wife, myself, and the girls would like to come out to your place this coming weekend for a visit if we can!"

Archie said, "Sounds good to me! Bring your fishing pole! All I have is a bunk house. I guess your granddaughter has told you! What's her name?"

"Dot," Matt said. "I will tell you the story later. I don't rough it anymore. I will bring my house!"

"I will look forward to meeting you! Why did you give us the money?"

Matt told him, "When Dot told us about your place, and what the people of the park are doing, I told her to write the check! I could not think of any place better to put it! I hope you can put it to good use!"

Archie said, "We will! We will use it to save our earth! We look forward to seeing you!"

Matt said' "Okay We will see you Friday about 2 P.M.! Bye now!"

Nikki had been listening! She said, "What do we have to do to get ready?"

Archie told her, "Nothing. We will save all the eggs we can for when they are here, and we will close the beaver pond for fishing! That is all I know of!"

Friday at two thirty they showed up with sixteen girls! Wanda the ex-con had tattoos from head to toe! Matt came with his wife Ann!

Wanda and the girls went to work picking what they needed for a salad! Nikki went with them. She wanted to know the plants that went in the salad! Matt asked Archie if he would like to try a drink of his whiskey! Archie said, "Yes!" Ann fixed them a drink of whiskey and water! They both drank it the same way! It was good whiskey!

Matt had the money. He said, "So why not drink the best?"

They started talking about the ranch and how nice and green it was. Matt said his was about the same. He had not planted fruit trees, but he was going to! Archie asked him about cows,

Matt said, "No cows. I have decided I do not like them anymore! I have a few horses for the girls to ride, They are the only grazers I have! Dot told me about the deer and Dustin. He sounds like a good man!"

Archie said, "Yeah, he is! We are going to hire him to manage the ranch and the church if he will work for us!",

The girls, some of them were taking off most of their clothes and wading in the beaver pond! "Picking something?" Matt asked him if he wanted to use the binoculars!

Archie said, "No! They seem to make it more cloudy when I use them! I can see pretty good some days! Today is a good one!" Matt asked if there was a spot where they could go to talk and be alone! Archie told him, "We could go behind the bunk house!" Matt said he had had enough of the girls for today. He knew they would be coming back shortly! Ann got them two lawn chairs and walked with Matt behind the bunk house! It was a warm day, but not to warm! When Ann left them with their whiskey and water. Matt started talking about his health. He said he had to sleep most of the way to the ranch. He said, "I am not feeling very good lately! My eyes have been bad for years, but there is something else lately! The doctors have not been able to tell me what it is!"

Archie told him about Toots, and what he had done for other people! He told him he was a witch doctor!

"When can I see him?"

Archie said, "I will have Nikki drive us in to the park tomorrow I will call him and make sure we can see him before we go!"

"What kind of fish do you have here?"

Archie said, "German Browns mostly! Do you want to go catch some?"

"Yes! But I will have to take my chair!"

"That's okay I have two of them already by the pond!"

Ann came out with Matt's fly pole and walked with them. She said, "I knew you two would not last long without fishing!"

Nikki and Dot showed up to help! Dot was Matt's eyes, Nikki was Archie's! Nikki was talking non-stop. After a little while Archie gave the pole to Nikki and said, "Shut up Private!" She did!

The only thing Dot would say was, "Now!" Matt would set the hook and land the fish! Dot would release it! Archie said nothing! Before long it was a contest. Matt had caught six fish. Nikki had caught five!

"This is not fair!" She said, "Two against one!"

Archie said, "I will be on your side Nikki! What do you want me to do?"

She said, "Talk to the fish they listen to you!" He started talking to the fish in a low slow voice! It's okay to eat the grey fly.

"Fish on!" Nikki said with a big smile in her voice!

Dot said, "It's okay to eat that brown fly mister fish! Now!"

Matt said, "Fish on!"

Archie said, "The fish say to get it out a little farther! Remember ten o'clock, two o'clock!"

Nikki said, "Fish on! He's a big one!" She started walking into the pond after him! She played him for five minutes before she could trick him into beaching himself! He was twenty inches, close to five pounds! Matt wanted to hold him. Dot took a picture!

Matt said, "You win Nikki!" As he pitched it back in the pond! "That's enough. I'm tired!" Matt said.

They went back to the house, it was dinner time. The girls had fixed baked salmon, fried potatoes, and salad! It was a good dinner! Matt went to bed! Archie and the girls built a fire and talked about life, what they could do to save our earth, they told stories and sang a little! The beavers worked to save our earth!

The next morning Archie called Toots and asked when they could come and see him. He said, "Anytime. Come to my trailer. I will be here!"

Archie drove the ranch road, but not too fast. Nikki asked Matt, "What do you do for fun?"

"Not much anymore." Matt said, "I used to ride horses with the girls, but I fell off once, my horse took me under a tree limb and it pushed me out of the saddle! I did not get hurt but I quit going!"

Archie said, "Write a book!"

Matt said, "I can't see!"

Nikki said, "You can talk. One of the girls will help you!"

Matt told them, "I don't know what to write about. I could tell stories about the girls, the ranch, and the oil."

Archie said, "I started with think sheets! Anything and everything I thought about! I would explain it to myself as I wrote it down!"

Nikki said, "When we get back to the ranch I will take you out to the beaver pond and read Archie's book to you! What we have so far, and read some of his think sheets to you!"

When they got to Toots place they all went in, what a mess! Books, magazines, papers, stacks of notes on the floor, the table, the book cases!

Toots said, "I am writing a book. It's a little out of hand right now!"

The tea pot whistled! Grandma came out with a tray and sat it down on top of a pile of papers and said, "You have got to do something or die!" She went back in the kitchen.

Toots asked Archie, "What do you think is wrong with Matt?"

Archie said, I really don't know, but I think it is a lack of exercise, depression, and too rich of a diet, and maybe too much booze!"

Nikki poured some tea. It smelled good! "Nuts, and apricots?" she asked.

Archie tasted his and said, "It tastes like raspberries!"

Matt said, "Cinnamon!"

Toots said, "You're all right! It has a green tea base, but I added the rest. Do you like it?"

They all said, "Yes!"

Toots asked Matt, "What do you think is wrong with you?"

"Well, Archie is right. I don't feel like doing anything most of the time! I don't eat the best! I drink every night! I sleep twelve to fourteen hours a night!"

Toots asked Matt if he could stay with him for a few days. "I want to talk to someone about my book, someone like you! I want to understand what you are going through! I can help you, but you have to change your life!"

"You know I can't see? I have to have my wife Ann to help take care of me!"

Toots said, "Okay we have room! When can you come back and stay?"

"Day after tomorrow!" Matt told him.

Toots said, "Okay bye!"

Matt said, "This is silly I am excited! This will be fun I hope!" As they got in the truck!

Archie said, "I want you to eat with Nikki and I tonight and in the morning is that okay?"

"Yeah. I am feeling better already!"

At the ranch that night, after the beans, and cornbread, with everyone around the fire, Matt told the girls what his plans were.

He said, "You girls know how to run the ranch! I want to start planting fruit and nut trees! I want overflows on the beaver dams! I don't know how long I will stay with Toots maybe a week or two! Call if you have to! You take the motorhome back to the ranch! Don't put off winterizing it! We will go out, all of us in the morning, to see how to install the over flows, and what kind of fencing to put around the trees! Ask questions! We want to get it right the first time! Everybody got hugs when Matt left the ranch the next morning. The girls made Matt promise to call if he needed anything!

Who knows who can conceive what we the people can do if we stop! Think! What do you believe, how have you been programmed? Is it over? Have we lost? Only if you stop trying to save our earth! More green is the scene. Get the beavers back! The Blue Sage!

Toots told Matt and Ann what the rules were when they got there! He said, "I will supply all the food! I will decide what drugs Matt can take! I will have a drink with Matt in the evening, we will go for walks, two or three a day! We will have oatmeal for breakfast every morning, and beans most nights! We will drink tea, lots of it! We will take H_2O_2 and apple cider vinegar every day!

Matt slept nine hours the first night. He woke up feeling good! They all had a cup of tea and went for a walk before breakfast! Toots started asking Matt questions about what he liked and didn't like about his life! Toots read his book to Matt and Ann. Grandma would listen in most of the time! Toots said, "I want people to understand we are in control! It is us, we the people that are killing our earth! I don't want to depress people, but I don't know how not to, if they see what we are doing!"

Matt said, "Tell them what they can do to help! How we can make a difference. Tell them what the T.P. of the T.P. have done! What you have done! The good things we are doing! Don't talk about the bad it is a better life for our grandkids! What we can do to change the earth! Toots said, "Yes, you are right! I think I am going to write for a little while! You and Ann should go for another walk! See you later, if you can, talk to the T.P. of T.P. on your walk it will help you!

They were gone for three hours. Eric got ahold of them and talked non-stop for two hours about his place and his book. Why he didn't rake leaves or pull weeds! Matt agreed with him, but he kept talking non-stop! He needed to talk so they listened! His place was like a jungle! No bare ground! He had fruit frees, nut trees, berries, a small garden! The water from his sinks and tub watered the yard! He had rain barrels on every corner of his home! The leaves were coming off the trees! He said he would not rake them!

It was good to hear how another understander understood! Walking back to the trailer, Ann said, "That's the first time I have really understood what you are talking about when you talk about saving our earth!"

Matt said, "Really? Why didn't you ask? I could explain it to myself as I tell you about it!"

"What exactly does the leaf litter do?"

Matt said, "Well, it's just like Eric said! When they are on the ground, they hold the moisture in so the bugs have someplace to live and something to eat. The worms and bugs aerate the soil! Break down the organic matter to feed the trees, grass, and plants. The aerated soil holds the water when the rains come or the snow melts!"

"Like a sponge!"

Ann said, "Yes! That's a good way to think about the beaver ponds, the bigger the beaver pond is, the drier it is, the bigger the sponge could be, miles across in some places!"

"You know beavers on the Mississippi river weighed three hundred pounds years ago!" Archie said that when they were on their way into town!"

Ann said, "Wow!"

"Let's go back. I am ready for a spot of tea and a snack!" When they got back the water was almost hot. They had dried apples and a kind of bread stick that had ten or fifteen different things in them! Like raspberries, sun flower seeds, dry fruit, nuts, and oatmeal, could be almost anything! You could eat them dry or with a honey or sorghum dip!

"A lady in the park made them in the fall she gets the kids that want to learn how, to help her then she vacuum seals them and freezes them, good huh?" Toots said.

"Well," Matt said, "This is working. I feel better than I did when I got here! Do you fish, Toots?"

"I haven't been fishing for years! I know a good spot if you want to go! I will see if I can find a ride!" He called the base doctor they had been friends for years.

He said, "Let's go tomorrow.My assistants can handle about anything that comes up! I have a phone. How about I pick you guys up at nine in the morning?"

Toots said, "Did I say there were four of us?"

He said, "No but that's fine. I have a big truck! Five of us will be fun!"

The doctors talked most of the way to the ranch! The base doctor said, "Yeah! I know they are doing all kinds of things with the eyes now! How long has it been since you've had yours checked?"

"Two years!"

"That's too long. Go to one of the new eye centers! They may be able to help you see again!"

Toots said, "I don't think so unless they can replace a lens!"

The base doctor said, "They do that now! Witch doctor Toots said I know they are doing amazing things, but I haven't seen it in my magazines! The only place I have seen anything about it is in. "The eye doctor. It's a pretty good read if you're interested!"

Toots asked if he saved them and if he could borrow the one about replacing the lens! The base doctor said, "Yes, Yes!"

Then they talked about Matts other problems that were going away. Toots talked for twenty minutes! He told about the change of diet, exercise, water, apple cider vinegar, T.P. of T.P., and how good they were doing, how healthy, how happy! Then they talked about gardening!

They got to the ranch at eleven o'clock. It was a race to see who caught the first fish! It was Nikki and she was late getting there, but she had her pole ready! She knew where to fish the shadows! Everybody caught fish, everybody had a good time! Everybody was happy!

Archie said, "We are having church day after tomorrow it will be cold! There is a cold front coming through! Dress warm!"

Well when they got to the barn at the Jone's ranch, Big Rown was there! He had a fire going that reminded him of his old preacher! Fire! Hot! Brimstone! He said, "You are going to die if you don't take some clothes off!" They did. There were great piles of clothes! Archie gave the opening prayer!

God grant us the mind power to accept the things we cannot change, the courage to change the things we can, and the wisdom to know the difference! No booze intended! Well it was just like Archie wanted! Everybody started talking in big groups and little groups! They all knew what they wanted and how to get it! That's the real question! Why should we want less green on the surface of our earth?

What's wrong with the U.S.? Think, who is in control? It could be the U.S. Everybody is watching what are you going to do? Save our earth! We can change! We can change our minds! What is really important? Being able to change your mind is a sign of intelligence! Change your mind! Think instead of watch, change your mind instead of play on your phone! What are we really doing? Please! Think! The beaver is working to save our earth!

Slowing your mind down. What a great thing to do! Yes! Stop and think! Why the hell would I want to kill our earth! I must not understand! What is going on? Why would we want to kill our earth?

CHAPTER THREE

The beaver was in the road! Standing on his hind legs! Rabies was my first thought! I stopped the truck! I was thinking about how good we had been getting along with the family. There were four of them now! Ma, Pa, Willy, and Nilly! That's what we called them, Kate and I! The beaver did not move until I got out of the truck, then he headed for the inlet to the dam! He went to their trail—there was in a trap! I pulled the stake out that held the trap in place and hauled mom out on the bank! I took the trap off her leg and let her go! She stayed on the bank for a long time! Resting! I think she would have been dead or bitten her leg off in the next ten minutes! I wanted to know who had set the trap on private property! The trap had a tag on it! The tag read, "Wildlife Management" and had a number: 21346! I would be able to trace it! It was hard not to think it was our government! I had been getting along with them lately too! When I got home, I told Kate the story and we went to the computer to look it up! Bill Gotems? Our neighbor? Hell, Bill did not set the trap; he has not been able to walk for five years! It had to be his grandkid!

"What is his name?" Kate asked.

Tom said, "All we ever called him was the little prick! I guess it is time to talk to him! The rotten little prick had better be nice or I will have him arrested!

"Wait a minute! What were you like when you were thirteen?" Kate asked. Tom did not talk for a few minutes. He was remembering! He had grown up wild and free mostly! He had gone from wild and free to six months in the hospital. He had lived with the Indians for two years. He had spent 30 months in prison! He knew he could not judge, but he would talk to him!

The next morning Tom was up at six thinking about what he would say to the little prick! Eric. That's it! Maybe I will remember, relate it now. I am America, King of the World! Tom thought at thirteen! I was going to be King of the World! I knew. I understood! (I wish!) I was beaten down enough to be insecure! I was not good enough at spelling, church, getting along with other kids! I was not easy to program—a trouble maker! I'll bet Eric has the same syndrome! I think Bill told me he was coming from Chicago! Trouble getting along there with school, church, and home. I will remember when we are talking. I think his dad died from AIDS. I will stay away from that until he wants to talk!

At 8 A.M. on Saturday Tom was at Bill's door! Bill was in a wheel chair! Bill said, "Eric has gone hunting! Would you like a cup of coffee? Come in! He helps me remember when I was young! Boy, was I a trouble maker! What did he do now?"

"Well, he trapped one of my beavers!"

"Oh shit! I showed him how to work the traps! I have not talked to him about it much. The beavers can help save our earth! They can stop the flooding in the Southwest, the plains, and everywhere all over our earth! What the hell is wrong with us? Why should we want to kill our earth? Sorry, I get carried away when I get talking and thinking!"

"It's okay. I liked it! I think we may be able to make Eric King of the World! If we think, talk, and understand together! What do you think?"

"Well, it will cause change! Change is good! Maybe it can work. Let's not go too fast. We don't want to overload him! If we keep it understanding and not memorizing. He will do fine! Who wants to fill their mind with shit that is already written down in a book?

Tom said, "Yeah! What if we were programmed to understand? Not memorize! What would our earth look like if we understood? It is us. We are in control! Think! Well, if I didn't know better. I would think we're both stoned. What the hell kind of a high is this? Understanding! That is how I think of it! I do it a lot! Now that I turned the T.V. off, I just sit and think! I write a few things down! I am starting to understand a lot of things! It is US! We herd the cows and we cut the trees that slow the breeze! We are the disease that is killing our earth! Bill, can I come back in about an hour with a tape recorder?"

"Okay, but I cannot tell you what I will talk about!"

"That's okay. I like to learn, understand, and see! I can tell you are beyond me in understanding. I want to listen. I am writing a book. You can help me if you want! I will be back in about an hour! I will have a cup of coffee with you when I get back!"

Eric came in the room. He had been listening to what we said! He asked if it was okay to stay on the back porch and listen when I came back. Bill told him, no. He would sit on a chair and listen and talk with us. That way he could ask questions when he needed to! When Tom got back, Bill and Eric had the kitchen table piled with all kinds of stuff. Two of the legs had books under them. They had oatmeal, matches, the tea kettle, a sponge, rags, what a mess! It was a good thing not to have a woman there! Bill was showing Eric how much water the beaver's dam could hold and how the area around the pond worked like a sponge to save our earth! Eric was having a good time listening and understanding. Him and Bill were having fun playing in the oatmeal!

Eric said, "I am sorry for trapping your beaver. I will not do anything to hurt them ever again! If you ever need any help with them. I will be glad to help!"

Tom said, "Well, I could use someone to help sometimes!"

Eric said, "Send a message by bottle when you want me to be where you want. I will be there! I walk the creek every day!"

Tom said, "Okay, I need to put an overflow on the dam by my house, or their dam will flood my home!"

Eric said, "Why wait? What time do you want me to be there?"

"Be there at 8 A.M. tomorrow!"

Eric was there at 7:30 A.M. ready to work! He thought he would be working on the edge of the pond! Not in the Middle! Why was he in the pond instead of by the bank? He asked Tom!

"The rocks in the center of the stream will keep the water from the overflow from washing away the banks!"

"Where did you get the idea for the overflow?"

Tom told him, "I read about them in an article! It had pictures. It's not hard to understand. The chain link fencing around the inlet stops the beavers from being able to dam the pipe!

Eric asked, "Can't they dam the chain-link? No!"

Tom said, "It's too big of a leak! And too little of a flow to hold the sticks in place. They try, but it does not work. They give up after a while!"

"How long do they live?"

"I don't know. I know Ma and Pa have been here for six years. They are bigger, but they don't seem any older! I will look it up on the computer and let you know!"

Eric asked Tom, "Is it okay if I come back and fish sometime? I seen a big one jump when I got here this morning!"

Tom said, "Let me and you give it a try when we get done with the overflow! When I moved here the biggest fish I could catch was about 6-inch! I have not fished here for six or seven years! There were no beaver here when me and Kate got here! I think there should be some big fish now!"

"How much more do we have to do before we are done?"

Eric asked, "Not much!"

Kate was yelling at them to come and get it! "We will be done in about an hour; we will come in then okay?" Tom yelled back. She went back in the house!

Tom said, "All we have left to do is put the chain link in and wire it to the posts!"

Eric said, "What do you think she has fixed us for lunch? I could eat the south end of a north bound skunk!" That's what my other grandpa used to say all the time! He always ate too much! He was big and fat! He died last year, he was a good friend! I miss him! That's when mom decided to ship me out here with Bill. I did not want to come. Bill was always kind of mean to me when I seen him before, but since my dad died he is much kinder!"

Tom said, "Well, I like tuna fish, I hope that's what we're having! She makes it with sweet pickles cut up real little, maybe a little onion, mayo and lots of lettuce! How does that sound?"

Eric said, "Let's go now!"

Tom said, "No. We will finish this first, then we will not have to put our wet shoes back on, we can fish bare footed, no shoes! Sounds fun! We used to, me and my friends, play at the park bare footed all the time! I miss them too!"

"How long have you been here and how do you like it?"

"Well, it's been about six weeks! At first I did not like it. Grandpa got out his 22 single shot one night and asked how I would like to have it! I wasn't sure and told him I have not shot a gun before! He said you will like it! We spent all night talking about gun safety, gun parts, how to clean it, how to take care of it! How to treat it like it was always loaded, never to point it at anything you did not want to kill! I will bet he said that 100 times! He told me a story about a friend of his who died when his cousin put on a gun and played quick draw. When his cousin came down the stairs, one shot through the heart! He said never point it at anybody or anything unless you want to kill it! He said his cousin was 17-years-old! Never play with guns! They are not toys; they kill things! Well, we went out on the front porch the next morning! It was fun. He had me set up cans, no bottles. 'We do not want broken glass,' he said! Well, he told me how it was done! How to line up the sights and how to squeeze the shot off! He did not miss! I did the first shot I took but that was all. After that I did not miss. He said to pick a spot on the can and to not shoot at the whole can! I have killed three rabbits and one squirrel, not birds! He told me after I learned what the birds are I could shoot some of them! He said to make every shot count; pretend it is your last bullet! Well, I have not missed a shot yet! We ate the rabbits. He said the squirrel was just a baby and not worth the work! I met a friend out hunting! I gave him gun safety lessons! He did not like it at first but he did do what I told him! I said I would not go hunting with him if he did not handle his rifle safely!"

Tom and Eric went to the house and started taking off their shoes. Kate came out and said they had to take off their pants before they could come in the house! "Women!" Tom said when she went in. "It's hard to live with them or without them! They have to control! If you learn this, you will do just fine with one!"

Lunch was just what Tom had said it would be! Good! Eric ate three sandwiches! When he went in the bathroom, Kate said, "Maybe I will have to buy more food. What do you think?"

Tom said, "Yes. He is a good worker, a good helper! I am going to ask if he will help me build my barn, shed, garage, or whatever it turns out to be! Maybe a workshop! I really need his help! I think it will be good for both of us!"

Eric came out of the John talking. "I don't have a fishing pole!" Tom said, "Wait a minute! Turn off the light, close the door, and turn on the vent fan if it is stinky!"

Eric said, "Okay, but I still don't have a fishing pole!"

Tom told him, "It's okay. I have 40 or 50 of them! I have been buying them at yard sales for years! I can remember when I was a kid. I did not have one. Me and my little brother had to share one! I had a hard time not buying one if it was a good deal, for years! I have one for you! Do you know how to fly fish?"

Eric said, "I know, '10 o'clock, two o'clock,' but that is all!"

Tom said, "That's okay. I like your honesty! I will show you. You are a bright boy! I like you and I hope you like me, us! I have a lot of work to do! I retire next month, so if you want to work, learn, and make a little money, let me know!"

Eric said, "Okay! I like you a lot! I can't believe you were not mad when I trapped your beaver!"

Tom said, "I was, but Kate reminded me of what I was like at thirteen. My dad left when I was seven! I kind of thought it was because of me. That's a hard thing to think when you're 8, 9, 10, and 11! Sometimes I still think I had something to do with it! I was a very hard kid to program, to do what you wanted, just because you said it was the way I had to do it! I had to understand, not memorize! I think you are the same way. I will not lie to you, and I expect the same!"

Eric said, "Okay. When do you want me to start?"

"Now!" Tom told him. "We will walk out back and look at supplies! I do not want to buy! I want to beg, borrow, steal; I want to use what can be re-used. I do not want to buy, order, build, like trusses I know they, whoever they are, are going to tear down the old movie house in town! If I can get the trusses for a good price, they will give us the dimensions for our foundation! It will be a big building—about 40 x 40. We will have to decide later! After we find our trusses! I have most of the uprights, walls, coverings; it was end cuts from that big tin building they built outside of town! If I use the end cuts like singles it will work! That is real recycling! What do you think?"

Eric said, "I think I will need time for all of this to sink in! You have obviously been thinking of this for months, maybe even years! I will need time to catch up!"

Tom said, "Okay, Eric. You are a smart boy! You think! You ask if you don't understand! You say what you think! Very good Eric!"

"Thanks. I think the same about you!"

An Interruption by the Author: How could you? Why would you? Who? Why? The two legged rats! The grazers! The rulers of the earth! Kill the beaver? Cut the trees? Over-graze? Why? Money!

They went to the garage. Tom was looking for fishing stuff. Eric was asking questions; "What's this for? Why is there a fishing pole with the fence posts? What do you do with this? What's. . . ."

Tom said, "Hey! Stop it! Think! I don't need ten thousand questions! Shut up! Think! Ask when you need to, okay? Do you think when you go to bed at night? If you do, think about this! Do I learn or understand when my mouth is open? And the correct answer is SOMETIMES, but think before you ask, please!"

Eric did not talk for a few minutes! Why ask so many questions when you could think? I know what that's for, a digging bar, shovels, that has to be a post hole digger. I have heard about them, but never seen one! Tom was right, think about it! He would not ask so many questions in the future! He would think!

Tom found his fishing pole by the fence post. Why was it there? Eric was being quiet! It sounded good. He was looking and recording his garage! That would be handy later! Tom thought, *I will find out how good his mind is!* After putting everything in the garage and using it for years. Tom knew where things were! He would see how good Eric did! This would be fun; a good test for both! It would let him know how he was! He did feel like he was losing it! His mind sometimes! What the hell are we doing killing our earth? Why? It sure as hell wasn't for us!

"Hey!" It was Eric. "Have you got what we need? Let's go fishing! I caught one when fat grandpa took us fishing once! He was fun before he got so fat! He had got in the habit of stopping at the fast food place whenever he could! He would take us kids along any time he could. He liked the high! I don't know what it was, but he liked it! The food? Feeling his arteries closing off! Feeling his mind shut off! I don't know what he was thinking, or how it felt! He ate there as much, as often as he could! He was only sixty when he died! But the fish! It was a cod. It was ugly, sixty pounds! It fought for a little while then I just dragged him in! Big mouth, not much room for a brain. Great big gut, just like Grandpa!"

Tom said, "Yeah. I have all we need, let's go! This will be good for you! Because you are bare footed, you have to be careful where you put your feet, so you won't spook the fish! The next time you go you will have shoes on, and you will spook the fish! You will see, learn, and understand! Let's go! I tied the flies on while we were in the garage! They are both the same pattern! We will see who does the best!" Tom caught six, Eric none. Eric said it has to be the Flys they trade poles, yep, Eric caught five bill one! They stopped fishing and started looking at how the flies looked in the water! One had a feather sticking out the back like a stinger. Yep, that's the one that only caught one fish! They cut off the stinger! They caught a lot of fish; they kept four of the biggest! One for each of them! Eric would take one to his grandpa! Trout like this were very good, even cold! After a little time on the barbie it would be delicious! Or, maybe the Japanese had the right idea with Sushi? Raw fish! I've had it it's pretty good! I have eaten the eggs out of a fresh caught brown before and I am still alive!

Sometimes it's fun to remember and think! Below the lodge would be good fishing now! He, Tom had closed it down years before when he saw the blue water running into a pure mountain stream! He called the E.P.A. and told them about it! Two weeks later the lodge was shut down!

Whoa! How strange! Eric and Tom had not said anything for minutes! He was understanding! How smart was Eric? How smart was he? He knew he was not one of the over-educated idiots controlling our earth! He knew Eric was not one of them! We will see what we can do! Let's think! What if we think instead of pray! *Touché*! Who's game is it, yours or mine? Ours!

Tom showed Eric how to clean the fish fast and easy! They took them to the house and showed Kate. She said she was going fishing for a few minutes. "Yell when the fish are done! I have baked potatoes in the oven and a salad in the fridge! I seen you catch, and keep one!"

Eric asked if it was okay to go with her. Tom said, "Yes. The fish will be done in twenty minutes, check your watch!"

Tom turned on the barbie and got the tin foil, butter, and seasoning out of the house! As soon as the fish were on the grill he got in the truck and drove down the road and picked up Bill. He said 'no,' but Tom would not take that; he picked up old Bill, chair and all, put him in the back of his truck, locked the brake on his chair and drove back to the house! Kate and Eric came over when they saw Bill in the back of the truck! Eric helped lift Bill out of the truck. Kate set up the picnic table! They did not talk much!

Old Bill said, "Watch!" He used his fork to pull the meat off the bottom of the fish as he picked up the fish by his backbone! He turned it over and did it again! He showed them the backbone and all the bones were still on it! Bill said, "I wish I could still fish!"

Eric said, "Why can't you?"

Tom walked in the garage and came out with a short piece of rope. He tied it to the front of Bill's chair down low and said, "I will pull. Eric, you hold the handles, don't push unless I tell you too! Kate, you get a pole! Let's go!

He pulled the chair with Bill telling him, "This is wonderful!" He said, "Mush!" once or twice with a smile on his face, and in his voice!

At the pond they watched old Bill! The first thing he did was ask if he could trim the fly a little. Tom said, "Go ahead. I'm here to learn!" He got out his pocket knife and cut most of the long parts off the fly! "Fish on!" he said on his first cast! His second cast, third, fourth, he caught a fish every cast! He was good! He said, "I still get my pole out once in a while and dry cast in my yard when no one is around! This is my first real fishing in five years! This is great! I guess some good can happen, even when it comes from a bad thing! We would not be doing this if Eric did not trap the beaver! How is she doing? Have you seen her today?"

Kate said, "No. I think with the two of you working on the overflow they are laying low today!"

"There's one!" Eric said, pointing at the overflow!

"That's Pa," Tom said, "Checking out what we did to the dam! I think she was not hurt too bad! She was strong and lucky! She would have died or lost her leg if the old man, Pa, had not flagged me down!"

"How smart are they Bill?"

"Smarter than us; they are working to save our earth! We are working to kill it! That's one of the things I understand now that I have stopped watching T.V.; I did not understand five years ago! I trapped and killed them for years! That's what I was paid to do by our government! Yep! Your tax dollars at work! Did you ever hear how I lost my legs Tom?"

"No. I think it had to do with an accident on the job didn't it?"

"Yes. We were taking out beaver dams with a cat, the cat was below me, I was standing on the bank above it! Watching one second! Then the ground gave way and I was, my legs, were under the cat the next! I screamed but it was too late, he was already on my legs! He pulled up, they had me in the hospital in twenty minutes, but there was nothing the doctors could do to save my legs. They were hamburger! The one thing I am glad of is my wife died that day; she never knew I lost my legs! She had cancer; she had been suffering for months! Hard times! But things are much better now; I have these new friends!"

It would be dark soon they had better get Bill back home! "Mush!" Bill said when Tom started pulling him back to the house!

On the way to Bill's house, Eric asked what time he wanted him to come to work the next day. Tom said, "I will stop by on my way home from work and pick you and your grandpa up, if he wants to come up! We can talk about what we will need to do before we start building! I will call and ask about the trusses! It should be early, about two P.M. I think! You forgot your fishing pole!"

"You never said I could have it!"

"Well, it's yours. We will find a few flies and leaders for you two! You and your grandpa! We will see what we can do about building Bill a four wheel drive wheelchair! How does that sound?"

Eric said, "Sounds good! I will tell him about it!"

"No, let's wait until we have a plan, he will want it too fast! We need to decide a few things first."

"Why can't we use an A.T.V.? That should work! Why can't we re-move the seat and make a new one special for Bill?" Eric asked.

"That is a good idea Eric! That will work! I will check on prices! Bill said the other night he has over $20,000 in savings! We can have him buy his own. He will like that better! Let's ask him about it tomor-row when he comes up! He will like it I'm sure!"

They got Bill out of the truck. He said, "I know I did not do much, but I am tired! I am going to bed! Good Night!" He wheeled himself into the house!

Eric said, "That's where I am going too! I'm tired. I will see you tomorrow and we'll talk to Bill about his new ride!"

Well, the next day Tom talked to the demolition company! Paul, the owner, said, "What a pain in my ass! I will see what I can do! $50.00 a truss. If I can save them without too much trouble!" Tom said he had talked to one of the old guys who had put them up! "I have a plan! Tell me when you are going to start! I will be there! If you have a good man at climbing and riggin' I think we can save a lot of good lumber and plywood! We are planning on eight A.M. Monday after next!"

"I will be there!"

He picked up old Bill and Eric at two P.M. the next day! They talked about the trusses until six P.M. Kate called them to dinner! Beans and homemade bread! Eric ate four bowls and a loaf of bread by himself! Bill said after Eric left, "Thanks for helping me feed him. I know what they mean when they say eating you out of house and home! I am spending five times more on food than I was before he got here! I have never seen anyone eat so much! Maybe he has worms?"

"I don't think so. I can remember eating thirteen hamburgers! Not very big! I was hungry! Anyway I am going to be there when they take down the old show house. I would like it if you and Eric could be there too!"

"I don't see why we can't! Can we go down maybe on Monday and look at it?"

"Yes! That's a good idea! I will set it up!" They did not talk about Bill's new ride!

On Monday they showed up at the old show house! When inside they could see how the trusses were bolted to the walls! They had Eric climb a ladder they had brought to see how hard it was going to be to take the bolts out! "Easy!" he yelled down. "Okay, we will take all the bolts out!"

Eric said, "All the bolts will be over 100!"

"I will help you. Let me know when it's my turn!" Eric started taking the bolts out, they saved any and all parts, nuts, washers, bolts, anything they could, they understood! They were helping to save the earth. They understood that if they did not have to buy; they were helping to save the earth! Think! At the end of the day they still had ten trusses to go!

Tom told Eric, "That's enough! We will come back tomorrow and do the rest!"

Eric said, "I can do them tonight!"

Tom said, "No! That's when people get hurt! We will come back tomorrow!"

The next day when Tom was undoing the last bolts, he found posters of Superman, Batman, and Wolf Man. He tossed a few posters down!

Eric said, "We're rich!"

"No. They are not ours! They are Paul's! Your granddad is right! He gets them! I will call him now to see if he has time to come by and get them!"

That day when Paul came by he said, "This is what I was hoping for when I got this job! We looked everywhere! I had given up! The trusses are yours free of charge! Do you have a trailer big enough to haul them?"

Tom said, "No, I was going to check into that today!"

Paul said, "I will haul them for free! Thank you for being so honest! I will not forget!"

When they hooked onto the first truss everyone held their breath! It came right out; no problem! The plywood fell to the floor! It was easy. They did not lose a single truss! The big track hoe was fast and efficient! The trailer was loaded before noon, half the trusses on the way to Tom's house with no way to unload them! He had not thought about that part of it!

When Kate saw the trusses, she went to the big elm tree with Tom's long chain! She had the truck driver back up until he was touching the tree with the trusses, she asked how many more were coming! The driver said, "One more load!" She had the driver hook the chain high and tight in the tree and to the bottom trusses! She knew as soon as the truck moved forward the tree would take the weight! Her dad was a logger, she had been taught how to hook, drag, load and unload! She stopped the truck when he had the trusses as high as she thought they would get off the ground! She did not know how to block them, so she would be able to use the chain for the next load.

Think Break!

Kate and the truck driver made a big saw horse, under the trusses! As he pulled out the saw horse held the trusses high enough to get the chain off!

Tom was ready to go home when the truck driver pulled in for the next load! The truck driver said, "If you ever want to get rid of your wife, let me know!"

Tom said, "No!" He knew he had a good one! He would see how she had done it when he got home! Paul asked if he wanted a load of plywood. Tom said, "Yes! That will help! How much?"

Paul said, "Looks like I will make about $100,000 off the posters, so it's your lucky day—or maybe payback time. Thanks again!" Tom asked Paul if he would put straps under the stacks of plywood. He was thinking he could use a come along and the big elm tree to unload it! Paul asked Eric if he had ever climbed trees!

He told him, "Yes! They used to call him the monkey man in Chicago!"

When they got home, Kate was fixing dinner; fish, corn on the cob and beans! Eric ate two trout, four ears of corn and two bowls of beans! He also ate three, maybe four slices of bread! Maybe he did have worms!

Tom told Eric, "All of the nails have to be pulled out of the trusses and the plywood! Don't hurt yourself! But that's what we need! And, if you can figure out a way to put the trusses up without renting a crane, let me know."

Think Break!

Well, when Tom got home the next day, Kate and Eric had a system going; they would tip the plywood on edge, hammer the nails from one side, lay them in the stack then pull the nails! He was amazed at how many they had done! Over half a five gallon bucket full of nails! He honked the horn, got out of the truck and said, "Fish break!" They went fishing. Tom asked Eric how his grandpa was doing.

Eric said, "I think he is writing a book! He wants to stay home! He doesn't even want to come over and go fishing when I asked. He is preoccupied! Consumed in thought! I think it's time to talk about his new ride!"

Kate said, "Let's go over and talk to him now!"

"Okay. The fish aren't biting anyway!" Tom said. They went to the truck! Bill did not look good when they got there; he said he was not feeling very good! "It may be what I am writing!" Eric grabbed the top sheet and read, *I understand it is us, the people of the Earth, over grazing, over populating, over cutting, over clearing, over cleaning, yes; it is US!*

Eric said, "Holy shit! No wonder you don't feel good! It may be true, but we have to understand it is 'US', not me or you? We came over to talk about something else!"

"What?" said Bill after a minute.

"Your four-wheel drive wheelchair!"

"What four-wheel drive chair? I don't know what you are talking about!"

Eric said, "We have an idea! How would you like one?"

Bill said, "Okay.. I think it sounds interesting what do you have in mind?"

Tom said, "Well, they have A.T.V.s with all the controls on the handles! Brakes, lights, gas, shifter, all on the handles! We can make a custom seat for your dead ass! What do you think? Maybe a bucket?"

Bill said, "No! I want a custom saddle! I know just the man to make it! Stinky Jones! He worked in the tannery when he was going to school. He cleaned all the meat off the hides before they went into the tanning process! He did smell bad! He fixes shoes, boots, saddles, any and all leather! I want to talk to him! I have not seen him in five years!"

"Okay. Can you go tomorrow? Eric and Kate are doing a good job of pulling nails! how about I pick you up at nine tomorrow? We will go find Stinky! It should be easy if the wind is in our favor!"

Tom said, "I think he has the same shop in the front of his house! He is a good guy! And don't call him Stinky!"

Tom asked, "What is his name?"

"Hell, I don't know! I can't remember! I don't know if I ever heard it!"

The next morning, Tom picked Bill up at nine. They went looking where Bill remembered it being! There it is: Stinky's Saddle Shop! I think it will be okay to call him Stinky! Tom got Bill's chair out of the back of the truck, helped him out of the truck and into his wheelchair. He did not need much help! I think he could do it himself if he had to!

Stinky was one hell of a nice guy! He had two employees. He said he had to have them; he was working eighty hours a week before he got them! "They are brothers. One can talk; one can't! They do good work. How can I help you?" he asked.

Bill said, "I want a saddle for an A.T.V. for me!"

"Sounds like a good fun project for me! We will have to make an imprint of your butt and what's left of your legs! Can you bring your horse by? It will have to fit him good too! How long do we have to make it?" Stinky asked.

Bill said, "I don't even have the horse yet! So don't fret! What do you think? A week or two to make it?"

"No. As soon as we get the print of your horse and your butt. I can do it in two days!"

Stinky told him. "Cool!"

"I'll be back! We're going horse shopping!"

Can you take an imprint of my butt today if I come back with a horse?" Bill asked.

Stinky told him, "Yes! We have everything we need! Buy a horse with a little spirit but not too much!

They looked at eighteen different A.T.V.s, but most were out of the question—too big, too much power, too much money! Tom said, "I will help with the money!"

"No! That is not it! I don't need an eighteen thousand dollar machine! I need something to run around on when I need to, to go fishing on when I want! I don't want something that will pull a car, haul a moose, or go 60 miles per hour, or climb a mountain!"

They were looking at three when Tom said, "I will sit behind you and help you stay in the middle if you promise to be good! What do you think? Want to take one for a test drive?"

"Hell yes! It sounds like fun!" Bill said.

"Shit you had better be good! No hot rodding! Okay?"

"Okay. I will be good. I will wait until I get my saddle!" Bill told him. The little two wheel drive with the small motor was all he needed! It handled easy, rode good! If he wanted to move up later he could!

They took it over to Stinky's. Bill had bought the loading ramp for it and some bags that tied on the front! When they came in the shop Stinky handed Bill a pair of plastic shorts and said, "We are all set up in the back! This will only take a couple of minutes! When it starts getting warm, you let us know. It gets hot fast! We have to get you out before it gets hot!"

They had a wash tub on the floor and rope tied to a rafter over the tub! Bill put on the plastic shorts, got in the tub. Stinky had two five gallon buckets of stuff, he put a chair on each side of the tub and told Bill, "When you get in the tub this time put your elbows on the chairs and do not touch your legs on the bottom of the tub!" Him and a helper poured the two five gallon buckets in the tub, and stirred it, it turned blue!

Stinky told him, "Okay. Hold still! Tell us when it starts getting warm, about 30 seconds!"

Bill said, "Okay." They helped him pull himself out, the shorts stayed in there, the helper was mixing more stuff! This time it was about five gallons total! When it turned yellow they poured it into Bill's imprint!

Stinky said, "Okay. We will let you know when your saddle is done!"

Tom said, "So, you pull his imprint out and make his saddle using that?"

"Yes!" Stinky said, "This is what they use to make custom legs, arms and even a helmet for bull rider once! He had to shave his head. He did not like that but he loved his helmet when it was done!"

When they got back home, Kate was fixing lunch. Eric was pulling the last of the nails out of the trusses! The plywood was stacked in one stack "103 sheets!"

Eric said, "That's almost 3300 square feet is that enough for your shop?'

Tom said, "I don't know. I haven't done any figuring on it yet!"

Bill said, "That is more than enough for your roof, but it won't do all the sides!"

Tom said, "I am thinking I will only heat about one third, the back third of the building. I will see how I want to do it as we build!" How long are the trusses?

"Thirty eight feet," Eric said.

Kate came out of the house and said, "Lunch is ready, chicken soup! I killed the old rooster, no more 5 A.M. alarm! I made tuna fish sandwiches too! The soup is really tasty, that old rooster did something right this time! Do you want to eat inside or out?"

Tom said, "Outside sounds good!"

"Okay! I will set the table. It'll be out in five minutes!"

Bill said, "If you ever get rid of Kate, I will take her off your hands!"

Tom said, "No, she is a good woman! She is a keeper!"

Eric said, "Let's help her set the table."

Tom said, "Eric, you go help her! She will like that!"

Eric ate three sandwiches again and his bowl of soup! His bowl was two times bigger than anybody else's! They gave it to him so he would not feel bad about the number of times he filled his bowl!

Bill asked Tom what his building was going to be. "Well," Tom said, "I weld and do woodwork. I like fixing things. We will park our vehicles in it! It's hard to say what it will be used for. I retire next month!

"What from?" Bill asked.

"Mining, I guess you could say, I am an engineer!" I did not go to school, but whenever they, anybody need to figure out how to do, fix, build, they come to me! My dad had a mine, one that had played out! But when the price of gold went up we did pretty good at it! We made anything we could not find used! We had water from the mine, we used water for power. It was a hard life, but a good one. I learned a lot more from him than I did in school! We quit and sold the mine when we found another vein! Dad was dying. He had bone cancer! He only lasted a year after we sold the mine! When we sold, the company that bought the mind offered me a job! I made more the first year working for them than I had in the five years before, and I had weekends off! That's when I met Kate. We were both out walking on a Friday night. Me because I did not like the bar scene, her because her car had quit! I gave her a ride back to her car! I removed the gas filter and put it on reversed! Had her turn the motor over and back washed out the filter! It was plugged! The car would not start. I had forgotten to put the coil wire back in. Kate had seen what what it was and fixed it while I watched! We talked until three A.M. she took me fishing the next day! We have been together over forty years! We did not have any kids. I don't think we wanted them. Our life was too good without them! It is okay? I have had a good life! Meeting you and Eric has been a good part in it! A very good part! What time do you want me to pick you up in the morning? Tom asked.

"Nine is good! We will be ready!" Bill said with a smile.

Well, Eric had not shown up for work for two days! He had walked home the other night, said he wanted to. He did not know why! He did not make it! He had not been to either place for two days! Not like a thirteen year old kid! The third morning, Eric was back at work! Bill was there! He said, "Where the hell you been kid?"

Eric said, "I met an old Indian out in the woods on my way home. She said she was out there to die! I asked her why? She said it was time! I asked her how she knew! She said she didn't! So I asked her why she was here if she didn't know? We talked all night, kept her little fire going, she understood what I said. I understood what she said!

Think! Think! Think! Stop the programming, the t.v. radio, I pad, phone, Computer! Think! Iti is us the grazers in control! Think! Eric the Blue Sage! Hell no, there is no end!

"What did you say at the end?"

"Nothing!"

"Yes you did! Eric the Blue Sage! That's it! Is that you? Is that what you said?"

"Yes, I have been for years, on a computer in Chicago! It was fun being a know it all! For other kids, if I really understood I would have told them how important it is to let green things live! Grow more, kill less green! Save, reuse, the economy is not important compared to saving our Earth! Think!

"Eric, do you know how smart you are?" Bill asked.

He said, "No! I think there are too many variables! Who knows? There are too many variables! Think! Eric, the Blue Sage!"

Bill had come up with some good ideas for the shop! He said, "If we have rain gutters on the shed, and rain barrels on every corner you will have water for your garden, trees, whatever you want. You won't have to pump the water out of your well!"

We had enough plywood to make the shop 24-feet x 38-feet; that was big enough for all Tom's wood working tools, his welder, his storage, and his junk! Kate would be able to park her car in the garage! She would like that!

Stinky called that night. Bill's ride was ready! He could pick it up in the morning! Tom was at Bill's at eight A.M.! "Your horse is ready to come home!" he said to Bill when he came to the door!

Bill said, "Let's go get him! Eric!" Bill yelled, "My saddle is done do you want to go get it?"

Eric said, "I am ready. If you're waiting on me you're wasting your time! Let's go!" They were at Stinky's at nine thirty. They, Stinky and Eric, set Bill on his new ride!

Bill said, "It feels like there is a rock under my left leg!"

Stinky said, "That's not uncommon. Show me where!" Bill showed him. Stinky got a knife and cut a hole in the bottom of his left stirrup! "How's that?" He asked as Bill put his leg back in the stirrup.

"Okay" Bill said. "Let's check the gas I want to ride it home!"

"No," Tom said. "You have almost ten miles of highway!"

Bill said, "It's okay; I will pay any tickets! I want to!"

"Okay. I will follow you!" Tom said. They did not make it half way there before the Sheriff pulled them over! He was a friend of Bill's! He told him the laws. "I will not bother you on the side roads unless you are doing things you shouldn't be doing, but you cannot drive it on the highway, understand?"

"Yes," Bill said. "I could get someone killed! Thanks Jim!" They loaded his mule on the side of the road! Bill liked calling it the mule, because it hauled his ass around!

Bill said in the truck on the road, "I am his worst nightmare! He will not like the day he hauls my ass to court! I understand. I won't lie! He will not like it!" At the turn off to Bill's place, Bill said, "I will see you in ten minutes! I want to fish! Okay??"

Tom said, "Yeah! Are you sure you don't need any help?"

"No. If you don't see me in fifteen minutes, come and check on me!" Eric asked about the A.T.V. spooking the fish.

Tom said, "We will find out!"

Bill said, "I will drive slowly!"

Bill was at the house in ten minutes with his fly pole and a beer! He said; "I wanted to celebrate! This is the first one I've had since Eric got here!" All of them went fishing! No hits, no runs, no errors! It had to do with the storm front passing through! Why should I, why would I want to do anything to hurt our earth!

Think Break!

It is us, we the people! We control, we decide, we want, we buy, we order, we build, we kill trees! We increase the breezes! We cause the problems our earth is having! Think! Please!

"I think I will like this a lot, but I don't want to catch all your fish! Do you know somewhere else I can go fishing?" Bill asked.

"The old cow rancher up the road has beaver ponds, now, he started letting them come back after I got mine. He is kind of an ornery old cuss, but he will let you fish, I think!"

"That's Joe! He's the man that was driving, skinny cat the day I lost my legs. It would be good to talk to him!" He always blamed himself. I tried to talk to him after the accident! He could not, or would not talk! It could have been him! We took turns driving the cat! He said it was his fault on the way to the hospital. I passed out before I could tell him it was an accident! I think I will go for a ride. Okay? What time do we need to be back for dinner? I hope!"

Kate laughed! "Six o'clock should be fine, but it is time to clean out the fridge. I'm not sure what we will be having—left overs of some sort!"

Eric got on the four wheeler with his pole, it was about five miles up the road to Joe's place! The gate was locked with a no trespassing sign on it! Bill told Eric to look for a key to the gate! "Look behind the gate post hanging on the nail!"

"Yep!" Eric said, "How did you know?"

Bill said, "Hell we worked together for over 20 years! We were good friends! We did all kinds of things for each other and with each other. He took care of my place when I was in the hospital! Ninety days! I had all kinds of infections. I had an old dog, chickens, a garden! He came to see me in the hospital maybe two times, he could not deal with it! He would tell me what was going on at work; and at home! He could only stay a few minutes each time! He would not talk about the accident!"

"I will shoot you! Who are you and what are you doing here?" Joe hollered!

"It's Bill, Joe. How much have you been drinking?"

"Too much! Come in. Would you like a drink? I was just going to fix me another! Whiskey and water!" Joe said; "Yes. I would like that; just like old times! This is Eric, my grandson. You guys will have to carry me! I don't have my wheelchair here!"

Joe chuckled and said, "Yep! Just like old days! I carried your skinny ass for twenty years, why should it be any different now?"

Bill laughed and said, "Good. I am glad to know you're still in there you prick!" He looked Joe in the eye and said, "Joe. It was not your fault! It was an accident!"

"Yeah, I know," Joe said, "but it has been hard on me!"

Bill asked, "Do you want to know what I have done so I could learn to live with losing my legs?"

"Yes!" Joe said, "I have learned how to think! I don't watch T.V. and I don't have a computer or a phone. I think!" Joe said. "Me too! I retired after your accident! I told them I could not skin cat, or kill beavers anymore! I said I was having nightmares! I was reliving what happened to you every night! I could not do it anymore! They were good to me! Gave me full retirement at sixty. I had over thirty years with them! This is my first year with S.S.I. money. I got an. $18,000 a year raise. It is nice to buy good whiskey! Here, try this!"

Bill said, "Do you have something for Eric to drink while we talk?"

Joe said, "Yes. What would you like Eric, soda?"

"No, juice, water or tea, no soda!"

"This is raspberry juice. I made it myself! After I got rid of most of my cows and got some beavers on the creek. I have an explosion of wild raspberries on the hills around the beaver pond and along the creek! I think it has to do with the water soaking into the hillside! What do you think?"

"Sounds right!" Bill said.

"Can I tell him about the oatmeal and match stick dam?"

"Yeah! If you want to. But make it sound like your idea, not mine!"

"Okay. I think it was a very good idea. There are the rags for the creek banks. You could see the rags soaking up the water as it came down the stream. You could see it slow the flow. You could see the oatmeal soak up the water when it got to the pond and dam. Bill told me how the trees are a part of the sponge how they suck up the water in the Spring, and how the beavers used the organic matter to make their dam bigger every year! Where did we think all the nice green valleys came from, if not from their dams? They can fix the earth if we let them. Help them save our earth. Think about it!"

Joe said; "I want to see it. Can we?"

Bill said, "Yes! But you have to clean up!"

"Okay. What do you want?"

"Rags, matches. Eric, go out and get a big double handful of mulch! We need two books under this end of the table! We need a big pan right there for the overflow, dam breakage, clean up won't be too bad if it is there. We need oatmeal! That's all we need I think! It will be good to watch you work once, prick!"

"Yeah. This is just like the old days! I do all the work and you sit on your ass!"

Bill said, "Good Joe. I am glad! Happy to hear you talk like in the old days! Now get to work. You have a job to do!"

"Asshole!" Joe said as he left the room. Bill thought, this is great! It will help all of us to understand better!

Eric came in with a double handful of mulch. He was smart enough not to close the door all the way when he left. He was a thinker! Joe came in with old pants, coveralls, but they were cotton so they would work! "Okay, Joe, I want you to put in the stream banks! Any way you want. Eric, you make the dam! Take your time, think! How can I make it stronger?" They used a pant leg across the lower side of the dam. They, Bill and Eric, knew the oatmeal would wash out if they didn't, they played flash flood! Drought! Spring rains, snow! Joe scraped some out of the freezer! They talked, they understood! It was fun to learn and understand!

Bill asked if it was okay to come back and fish! Joe said, "I get to go! I haven't fished since the last time we went—you remember? When you closed the lodge? The blue water?"

Bill said, "Yeah. I was thinking about that just the other day! That should be good fishing after this long! Oh shit! I forgot! There is a storm front coming through! We had better go!"

Eric opened the door. It was already raining! Bill said, "It's okay. I have over sized garbage bags on the front of my mule! Eric, go get them!"

Joe said, "This is just like the old days. You never did have a rain coat!"

Well, they made it home just when the skies opened up! The rain came down like someone had opened the flood gates! Rain drops a foot long with a one inch diameter! "Just like a tall cow pissin' on a flat rock!" Bill said. "That's what my grandpa used to say!" They watched the rain in the porch light! Eric got Bill's wheelchair, helped him get in it. They had cold cereal and went to bed!

The next morning, Tom was at Bill's door at eight A.M. checking on them! He said there had been a flood, his yard had been flooded when he got up! He did not know if the road would be washed out or not! He had to go to work and told them if the road was washed out he would be back!

Bill started cooking breakfast of eggs, hash browns and toast. Eric got up and said, "Boy, what a good night sleeping! I don't think I moved all night! Who was here?"

"Tom! He said his yard and his place were flooded!"

"After breakfast let's go check on Joe!"

"I like him. I hope his place is okay!"

"I want to be able to get off my mule without you helping me. I think a rope tied to the rafters in the car port should help. It should work! I have all kinds of rope in the shed out back. Why don't you go out and get a fat soft one. You can tie it up before we go. I will see if I can get on my mule without any help!" Eric brought back a one inch cotton rope! He said, "I think two ropes instead of one is the way to go! You don't want to be swinging around. Two ropes will keep you stable!" He stood on the mule and tied the rope where Bill told him to tie it! A loop hung down over the chair and the mule. Bill grabbed the rope and lifted himself out of the chair and into the saddle quick and easy! "

Yep!" He said. "Let's go. Don't forget we left our fishing poles at Joe's!"

Joe was in the house with a squeegee pushing water out of the door! He said, "It's been close before, but this is the first time it has been in the house! I will have to take out the beavers dam I guess!"

Eric said, "No! All you need is an overflow! I will help you put it in. We did it at Tom's place. It works!

Joe asked, "What kind of overflow?"

"It's a big pipe on top of the dam with a chain link fence around the inlet, so the beaver cannot plug the pipe! It's easy. We can do it today. We can use that big culvert over there."

Bill said, "Not today. It will be much easier after the water goes down!"

Joe said, "You said the other day Tom was building a big shed! I want to see it and the overflow on the beaver's dam. I will get my four wheeler! It's a big one. Eric can ride behind me if he wants!" Well, Bill took off like the nut that he was in the old days! Joe did not try to keep up! He told Eric Bill was always the first one there, always the fastest driver, always going faster than he needed to! It was a wonder he had not wrecked more than once! Eric said, "Let's go back. I forgot to get the fishing poles!" Joe drove back to the house. Eric grabbed the poles!

Kate and Bill were talking when they got there. "This is funner than recess when I was a kid!" He said when they pulled up.

Joe said, "You had better think about a truck coming around a turn driving the same way you are! Practice stopping, See how you can get out of their way. I don't want to come see you in some hospital—or or to your funeral!"

"Yeah, you're right!" Bill said. "I don't want to go to either one!"

Eric said, "You can see the overflow from here, we can look at it closer after it dries out! Let's talk about how we can put up Tom's trusses. Has he got a plan yet Kate?"

"No. He says he doesn't know yet! He can get the big track hoe from Paul or a crane from work, but he doesn't want to use either one. He says I will figure some way to do it! He says I know my dad would come up with a plan! I will!"

Joe said, "All we have to do is get one up! We can brace it, tie it, and use it to put up the next, one at a time!"

"Let's put up an "A" frame on the back, we can take it down after we get all the trusses up!" Eric said.

Kate said, "He has a big old block and tackle! I think I know what Eric is talking about. I will get some paper and a pencil!"

"Tom will be impressed if we can come up with a plan to put them up!" Bill said.

Kate got a paper and pencil. Eric started with a simple "A" frame on the back wall.

Bill added two braces to make it more stable. Kate ran the long chain to the apple tree out back. Joe made a little "L" brace at the top of the frame to hook the block and tackle to.

Joe said, "It will work!"

They, mostly Eric and Joe, built the frame on the back wall! Eric was a monkey man on the top of the walls. Kate kept saying, "Be careful!"

Eric, after a while, stopped working and asked Kate to be quiet. He said, "I am being careful! You're not helping! Let me work please! Bill's mule would not drag the truss, but Joe's would. Kate drove! When they tied Bill's mule to the block and tackle it picked the truss up no problem! Kate did the ground rigging and checked the bolts on the plates on the truss joints! It was up and in place with very little problem! Eric drilled the holes. Joe bolted them in place.

Bill said to Kate, "If you bring your fixings outside, I will make sandwiches!" She did and he did. They had lunch and admired their work! Bill said. "If we build it right, we can set each truss in place with no hassle! Here. I will show you with the pencil. He drew a jig that fit under one truss and over the next! The 2 x 10 they used was just the right length with 2 x 4s nailed in the right places at the right angles. It held itself in place! The trusses went up fast. The drilling and bolting took time, but at 4:30 they had six trusses bolted in place with cross braces in place so they would not move with the wind!

Tom sat in his truck. Bill brought him a shot of his whiskey and said, "Here, we are celebrating! What do you think? Kate is fixing dinner! We told her we could go home. She said no, she wanted us here when you got home!"

Tom asked, "Where's Eric?"

"He's fixing dinner with Kate." Joe walked over to the truck. "Well, what do you think?" he asked.

"I think I owe you guys! What do you want?"

"I think we both need a woman like Kate! Can you do that?" Joe said, jokingly.

"What else do you want? If I ever do find them, I will let you know! But, I don't think I will! This is great. I have been losing sleep! For some reason, I could not come up with a way to get them up there without using a crane or a track hoe! Who thought of the "A" frame on the back wall?"

"That was Eric! He is a very smart boy! We all had ideas that helped. We used them all! Bill and I have another idea. We want to help you buy Eric a mule like Bill's, for his fourteenth birthday at the end of this month, the 29th!" Joe said.

Tom said, smiling, "That's a great idea! Let's have Stinky build him a custom seat too! Just for kicks! We can have it here on the 29th. A surprise party! We will tell Kate when Eric is in the bathroom after we eat!"

Kate opened up the door and said, "Soup's on!" It was mostly canned stuff; corn, peas, green beans, a bottle of deer meat, and canned stew of some kind! Homemade bread, fresh out of the oven. Bill wondered how she had found the time to do that.

They—Eric Joe and Bill—said, "We will be here in the morning to put the rest of the trusses up!"

Tom said, "No! It's not a busy day at work tomorrow; I will come home early. I want to watch, to help. After all, it is my shed!"

Eric asked Bill, "Does it feel good to be out of the saddle?"

"No!" Bill said. "I like it! It's the best seat I have ever had! It is very comfy!"

"Do you guys want to come over and shoot a game of pool after we get Bill's table repaired?"

"What's wrong with it?" Tom asked.

Eric said, "Well, it's not level! There is a bump where the slats come together! You know 1/3 of the way up or down! And a little bump on the other end!"

"All you have to do is level it!" Joe said.

"Really?" Eric said.

"Yes. If you spend enough time it will work!" Joe told him.

The next morning, Bill had Eric get a piece of plywood, the floor jack, a 2 x 10 and two 2 x 8s that were long enough to use under the table and a few blocks! They could lift the table up high enough to move it a few inches. They moved the table to where they wanted it, started leveling it, but it took some time! Tom showed up at 10 o'clock! He walked in on them when they were getting close!

"Ready to work?" Eric said.

Tom said, "No, I want to know what's going on!"

Eric told him, "We are leveling this pool table!"

"Why don't you use water?" Tom asked.

Eric said, "How?"

Tom told him, "I have what you need at home! I have a clear hose that will work perfect! We can use colored water in it! I will give you some and I know Kate has food coloring. We use it at Easter time! So, you guys can stop playing for now and get to work!"

Whose game is it? Mine? Yours? Ours? Who is in control? Who is studying the rats? US! Think! It is us; we the people are in control! Think! Please! Save the green! Green is King! Save our earth! Get the beavers back!

Well, at the shed, Tom said, "I thought I was good at figuring out problems! You guys are great! You made it easy! Thanks! I will not forget! I don't mean you did not have to work, but we did not need a track hoe or a crane! Thanks! That's the way I wanted it! I know it is us we are in control! I know we can use less, buy less, recycle more, grow our own more! Save our earth! The economy is not that important if we are talking about saving our earth!" They were done putting up the trusses at 5:30 P.M.! Kate had steaks on the barbie!

"Well, I know I have said it lots already, but thanks you guys! If you stop helping me it's Okay! If we never stop helping each other I will love it! You want that hose so we won't forget? Yes! Kate, do you have some food coloring? Tom said you might!" "I have red or yellow! I don't use either of them! " "Either one will work! Thanks!"

"Let's see, I know the hose is here! But I can't remember where!" "It's behind the fence post!" I remember, he was right! I remembered after seeing it! Programmed am I? Yes! Are you? Yes! We all are, like it or not! Yes! You can change. I have! I have stopped watching most T.V. I do not listen to the radio when I drive. I have not hooked my computer up in over a year! Programmed? Not as bad as I was! Think! We are all doing what "they" want us to do! Kill our earth! Money! Yes!

At the pool table the next morning, Bill filled the hose half full of yellow water and put it on the table. You could see the north east corner was low. They put the floor jack under it, raised it until it was a little high, then slipped some playing cards under it! "We will check it in the morning!"

They would check the table when they got back from working on Tom's shed. Joe had just pulled in when they got there. "Let's go look at the overflow!" Joe said. "I want to do mine before we get another flood!"

"Okay. You going?" Bill asked Eric.

Eric told him, "No. I am going to think about how to get the plywood on the roof!"

At the overflow Joe said, "I wish we would have thought about this in the old days! Instead of killing the beavers and taking out their dams!"

"Yes. It would have been a lot better! It shouldn't be hard to do this at your place! Eric will help you just let us know when you are ready!" They went back to the house.

Eric was working on building a swing crane he said, "It's Kate's idea. Look at the drawing on the picnic table!

They did and said, "It looks like it will work to us! What can we do to help?"

"Build it!"

Eric said, "I will find a pulley and a rope!" Eric came back with a trailer hitch and a ball first. He said, "Can we use this?'

"Yes," Joe said. "Good job!" He walked over to Tom's scrap metal pile and found what he needed! Two pieces of steel and one 4-inch angle. He went to Tom's welder. In ten minutes he came back and started drilling and bolting the pivots to the 4 x 6 they were using for the upright on the crane! Bill was using his mule for a saw horse! He was cutting the lumber for the braces they needed. Kate was his assistant! It was lunch time when they got the first piece of plywood up! Bill talked about how important it was to keep it square! Bill used his mule to raise it above the trusses, then Eric and Joe set it in. place! Tom had put a chalk line where they needed it after they had squared the walls. They only put a few nails in the first four sheets to make sure the lay out was right! It was! Tom had done a good job!

"Lunch!" Kate yelled.

They came over to the picnic table. Peanut butter and raspberry jam. They made their own and ate without much talk! Kate said she had to go shopping! They were running out of food! Joe said, "Come by my house first I have a lot of stuff, food I am not using! Let's have dinner at my house. You can look at what I have before you go shopping! I will leave early so I can be ready to feed us at about five thirty." The way it should be! "Traders" Yes!

Tom got home about two thirty and said, "Stop work on the shed! There is another storm coming. We are going to Joe's place to put in his overflow."

Eric said, "I will be down in about ten minutes! I want more nails in the plywood before we leave!" Tom got his chainsaw, axe, post pounder and chain link loaded it in the truck! Eric was down and ready to go! Bill had already left. When he got to Joe's he was in the kitchen starting dinner! He said he was making soup!

Bill took over, told Joe his helpers would be here in about ten minutes. "Tom said he would bring post, ax, chainsaw and chain link! Can you get the culvert over to the dam by yourself?"

"Yes! All I will need is for you to help me get my chair off the back of the mule!" Bill said. "What's your plan for the soup?"

Joe told him, "The roast is in the fridge; veggies are on the table! Use the drippings in the roast pan for the soup. It should cook fast in the big pan on the table! Watch it, it will boil over! Turn the heat down low, just so the lid rattles! I would get the carrots cooking first, then potatoes, zucchini just before you serve! See ya!"

"Have fun!"

Bill said, "I would rather go with you!"

"I know," Joe told him.

At the pond Tom showed up first! He looked at the dam and said, "The overflow goes right here. Bring me the chainsaw!" He used the chainsaw then the axe! The water was running out! He understood. He knew what he was doing! Eric watched! He was learning!

Tom stopped working! "I don't know what we can do without the pipe!"

Eric said, "I do, we can put in the chain link!" He got the posts out of the truck, put them in where he wanted them and started wiring the chain link in place! He had done this before, he understood!

Joe came dragging the pipe over with his four wheeler! Joe said, "Still moving, are you ready?"

"Yes!" Tom yelled! Well Joe pulled the culvert up perfect! They rolled it into place! It was running water through the pipe as soon as it fell into place! The beavers would fix the leaks! Think! They want to save our earth! Why help the cows eat it! Think! We the people control! Someone was yelling at him. Eric!

"That's good enough! It will work! It's time to eat!" See! I told you as soon as you said food he would pay attention! Just like my dog! Do you think we are programmed?

Well, Bill had the soup done, but he was not happy! He said he had turned his back on the pot for ten seconds and it had boiled over! Joe said, "Yeah, I know, it does the same to me! I can't understand!"

"I know!" said Eric. "It is like a pressure cooker! If something is cold in the pot the heat goes to it! To expand it! When this is done it boils over!"

I understand. Can you? Will you? What if you do! Will you do anything to fix it? Can you save our earth? Can we save our earth? The beavers can save our earth! Please think!

Kate had brought some homemade bread to go with the soup! The soup was very good, rich! After dinner she and Joe loaded a lot of food in Tom's truck! Mostly canned goods from the house! With carrots, potatoes, onions, cabbage, and a ham from Joe's root cellar!

The next day Tom was home. They started on the shed at eight thirty. The plywood went on fast! They used the crane to put the tin on the roof! It was cloudy out. Tom took his shoes off to walk on the roof.

He said, "I have done it before! I don't feel like I am going to slip when I am bare footed!" Eric took his shoes off too. Joe had new tennis shoes. He left his on! Tom had some very good screws for screwing the tin down. They went in very easy. All three of them had cordless drills. The tin pieces were three-feet six-inches long and went on fast! They got a little rain at about two P.M. Tom ordered everyone off the roof! "We had a man fall and break his back last year at work. It was a wet tin roof! That's not going to happen here! Get off now!"

When they were in the shed Kate asked Eric about the old Indian he had talked to! "What was her name? Chowwagutes? Something like that!"

"That was her Indian name! We did not talk about what it meant! We talked about what the country was like before the whites came. Her grandmother had told her how good it was, how many beavers, how many fish, birds, animals, and how green! Yes! She knew how primitive the Indians were! They took a lot better care of the earth, "Mother Earth," than the white man did! She said that we are killing Her. We are draining the water out and off our earth! The water that keeps Her alive; the water that feeds the trees, the plants; it goes into the seas in floods, just like flushing a toilet! She talked about the bees, the trees, the seas, the disease that's killing our earth! US! This is what I thought when I listened to her, not what she said! Sheeple, the two legged rats, the two legged talking goats, the controllers! US! It is us! Why are we killing our earth? Why? To have a better house? Car? Boat? Wife? Paycheck? Hunting, or fishing trips? You are programmed to do what you do!" Think! Eric, the Blue Sage!

Everybody was looking at him when he stopped talking! Kate had started clapping when nobody said anything!

"Very good Eric! How smart are you?"

"Too smart and not smart enough!" Bill said. He said he did not know! Too many variables!

I am starting to understand that most of the variables are caused by us! We control, we buy, we create the demand! We burn. We kill the green! We herd the sheep that are killing our earth! It is us! Think! Why do we do what we do? The only reason I can come up with is, WE DON'T UNDERSTAND! We are programmed to do what we do! We can't understand and keep doing what we are doing and survive! Think! We all of us think! "You Eric, should be King of the World! What do you think of that?" Bill asked. "I think I might like it! I think I might be able to save our earth if I were!"

Nobody talking.
Everybody listening.
Why aren't we like he?
Totally understanding!
Totally honest!

Totally knowing, right all of the time! What was wrong with us? Why do we keep doing what we are doing if we understand? Drugs in our water! Something to keep you under control! Comes in your hamburgers! Something to keep you the Sheeple, we are! In your education! In your church! In your job! Your programming! To help you get along! I think yes! What? Do you the reader think? Let me know! Eric, the Blue Sage!

We the controllers are in control! We decide what kind of an earth our grandkids will have! Please think! What do we the people want? A greener earth can save us! Our grandkids! We are an experiment! Think, please! Eric, the Blue Sage! Save our earth! Think!

This time everybody clapped! Tom said, "There is good and bad in all things!"

"Yes!" Eric said.

"You are a very smart man! When I think about the oatmeal beaver ponds and what holds a real beaver pond in place, I wonder again how smart are they? Bill or Joe?"

Joe said, "They can be pretty dumb in some ways, but when it comes to flood control, or flood irrigation, they are the masters! We should watch, think, and learn from them!"

"Bill, I thought about how their dams were made and why for years! I saw one after a long dry spell! It was like brick on the back side, the sun had dried it, and the pond was real low. The beaver were putting in their winter food supply just like they always did! We had a flash flood a few days later! Their dam held! It stopped a lot of water! Joe is right! We should watch and learn from them!"

Kate started talking, "My grandpa told me they were bad. He said they eat the apple trees. They flood my yard! They are bad! The cows get stuck on their dams! Or around them!"

Eric said, "How long have the cows been here?"

Tom said, "Three or four hundred years! The beaver, a million! Give or take a few!"

Bill said, "I don't know if they understand! But they can and will help to save our earth if we let them!"

"Bill is right!" When the spring rains come down the creek, they do everything they can to make the flood plain bigger! I think they know, the more they slow the flow, the greener our earth will be! The bigger and better their dam will be, the better their life will be! ALL LIFE!

Eric said, "So they know how to make it a better life for all! Yet, we don't let them? They know the more organic matter on the surface of the earth the better for our earth! The better off all living things will be! Organic matter holds the moisture! To cool the breeze! To save the trees! To stop the disease that is killing our earth! Where do you think we are going if not to hell? If we don't change our ways! We are turning our earth into a marble! Another, bigger Mars! It is not a big bang! It is a slow moving disease! Killing our trees, filling our seas, we can cure the disease! We can plant more trees! We can help the beaver slow the flow to the seas! Think! We can help beavers stop the flooding, we can put overflows on their dams! We can help them save our earth! They work to save the Earth! What are you doing? They work to save our earth for nothing! How much do you charge for killing it? $10.00 an hour for killing the green in my yard! $20.00 an hour for a digger, a back hoe! $60.00 what for, to kill more green? To make more bare ground! Wake up! Why? Who for?

We, us, you, me, thee? What do you think? Can you plant a tree? Can you see, it is us, you! And me! We can save our earth! Please help the beaver come back! Think!

"I don't know about you guys, but I am on overload! Let's go to Bill's and shoot some pool! I don't care if the table isn't level! It is the same for everyone!"

"Okay," Someone said. They saddled up and rode out! On the way Bill drove slow! He was thinking what if we slow down, drive slow, buy less, think more, understand more! Not watch so much T.V. and not play so many games!

Someone came around a blind corner pulling a horse trailer. They ran Bill off the road! He went down a twenty foot embankment and into a beaver pond! Bill was swimming when they came back looking for him!

He said, "This is not bad! Come on in!"

Kate asked, "How's the water?"

"Cold and wet! Get me out of here!" They made Bill tie a rope on his mule before they would help him out of the beaver pond! The bank was too steep to climb without ropes! Kate had three set up! They put Bill back in the saddle! Pulled him and his mule back to the road!

Tom said, "You rode him down, you can ride him back up!" When on top, Bill asked Joe to take the air cleaner out of his mule! Unbelievable! His mule started right up! Bill asked if someone had a dry shirt he could borrow. Tom had one in his truck!

At the house Tom said, "I have an idea for a new game! We can all play! It goes like this. You rack anywhere you want as long as it is in the rack! You shoot until all the balls are off the table 10 to 30 shots, who knows! It is a new game!"

They said, "Okay. You go first so we understand what you are talking about!"

Tom racked the balls in the corner pocket! He made three, oh yeah! A scratch ball is a ball in hand! He said, "If you knock the balls or the ball off the table you get counted two strikes! The lower the number of shots the better!"

Eric watched and thought! He had never shot pool before but this was the third person in front of him! He could see which shots were good! He could see that a nice easy stroke made the shot! He could see that anything was an interruption! This looks like fun, he thought! Well just like everything else, it took a little time to learn! He shot a twenty. It was his first game ever! First time on the pool table!

Kate asked, "Eric, where did you learn to shoot pool?"

"This is my first time ever!" Eric said. Everybody said, "Bullshit!" at the same time. Eric said, "I watched three players before me. I saw that when they line up the shot properly, they made the shot! I could see that any distraction would cause them to miss the shot!"

No mind is better than the fantasy! Think! What if we the people really tried to save our earth? We could! What could we do? Think! That's all I ask! Eric the Blue Sage! Think! It is our earth! We are in control! It is us! Think! What can you do to save our earth! Buy less, use less, drive less, grow more! Kill less green! Think! Please! Eric the Blue Sage!

Tom on his second game shot a sixteen. Bill took the arm rests of his wheelchair, he shot a seventeen. Kate shot a thirty one. Eric shot a sixteen he looked like he had been playing for years!

"How could anyone be so good so fast?" Kate asked Eric.

He said, "I remember watching a game on T.V. I played marbles. I don't know, but it looks very easy and it is for me!"

Kate said, "I am going fishing, can I borrow a pole from someone?"

Bill and Eric said, "Yes!" at the same time. Kate took the little box of flies and leaders. They, the guys, had fun playing and talking about the shots! They were not keeping score very good anymore! They were shooting, practicing their English! Learning from each other! It was not hard to see that Eric would be king of the table before long! When Kate got back the guys were in the carport in lawn chairs, talking about Bill's wreck.

"Who ran you off the road?" Joe asked.

Bill said, "I don't know! It was a white truck and trailer! I did not have time to get his tag number! I don't think I want to know!"

Kate had four fish, two were big ones, 18 to 20-inches! Eric wheeled the barbie out from in back of the house. Bill and Kate went in the house to find fixings for the fish and something to eat with the fish! Mac and cheese is what they fixed! Bill had sourdough biscuits. Bill opened two cans of corn, dinner was served!

They ate without much talk, that's the way it always is, if the food is good! After dinner, Eric asked where and when Bill, Joe and Tom had played pool before. "Tom's! It was his dad! They, him and his dad would go to the pool hall any and every time they went to town! 1, 2, 3, 6 or more hours depending on who was there. My dad was a hustler! We would con newbies that came into the pool hall! He would pretend to be, or get drunk! I am not sure which; he would win money! Sometimes a lot! I watched him take this fancy dude's Rolex one night!"

Tom said, "He knew what he was doing! He lost $300.00 before he took him! He told this guy he was a gold miner! That's all it took! Dad even fell on the floor once! He took this guy hook, line and sinker! He had a little pouch in his vest pocket with six shot you know! Shotgun BBs in it! He put it in my hand and said.

"Here! You hold it! Give him yours!" Me and my dad did not know each other as far as the dude knew! The watch too! I was just a dumb kid watching! My dad made five balls on the break! The dude exploded!

He said, "What the hell was that? You are a hustler!"

My dad said, "Well, so are you! You were going to take some old drunk guy for his money and gold weren't you?"

The guy said, "Yes!"

Dad said, "Okay! We understand! Because it was your dad's watch! Because I knew it was my game and I would win, I will give the watch back and no hard feelings!

The guy said, "Okay! You will be back on top in no time! I was trained to go out back when he broke! I had seen it before! One guy tried to hit him with his pool cue. My dad ducked and went over the pool table like a shot! He lit on top of the guy and choked him out in ten seconds! But I always watched the game! I know how to play!

Thanks you guys! This is a fun game! The overflows! The shed! The pool! This is a better life lately!"

Bill said, "Well, mine is a little different! I was raised on one! I had an uncle that used to babysit me when I was a baby! He would put me on the table, he would teach me not to throw the balls! Not to bang or drop the balls on the table! He taught me respect for the table! I still have that, and I always will! I did not play much as I got older, but I still like the game!"

Bill did not let the loss of his legs bother him too much! He knew it was what happened and he could not go back and change it! He had to live with it or die! He said, "Thanks you guys! This has been great lately! I like to feel like I am doing something! Helping someone!"

"No!" Joe said. "I am sorry but I am not ready yet! I do like my life better lately, but I am not ready!"

Kate asked, "How would you guys like a drink of Bill's good whiskey?"

Eric said, "You know I saw what booze did to young mind in Chicago when I was growing up! I saw a friend die. He drank too much! He was only eleven, he did not know what he was doing! Just like us! We the two legged rats don't! Understand! What we are doing! Killing our earth! We kill! The trees! We think we have controlled burns! We clear the land! We over-graze! Think! Are the cows the rulers? Think! The grazers are eating our planet! People! Goats! Sheep! Horses! Cows! We are eating the thing that keeps our earth alive! The green is the thing! Think! Eric the Blue Sage! Think! Please! Do you think of yourself as well educated, or over-programmed? Think!

If I do no piss you off you are not alive! Think! What are we the people of the Earth doing if not killing Her? Why? Who for? It ain't for the beavers! They are trying to save Her, our earth! People, the plants, for the cows! We the shepherds we herd them, the grazers, we tend them! They are eating our earth! We mend them! Think! Who is in control if not us! We the people! The grazers! Understanding. I am almost there. I think! Too many variables! Yes! Bull's eye!

CHAPTER FOUR

Tom came home from his last day at work as a steady employee. They wanted him to work part-time as a consultant! He told them he would! Part-time, he had said—Eight or ten hours a week, no more!

Kate came out of the house and asked if he felt different! He said, "Yes! We're going to church!"

"Not me. You know how I feel about that!"

"I want you to listen then decide!" He waved at Eric & Bill to come over. They were putting tin on the walls of the shop.

"I am going to church on Friday night; you guys want to join me?" They both shook their heads no, but did not say anything!

"This is the Church of Universal Understanding! No preacher, no suits, no ties. Mostly cowboys and old people, from what I understand! The man the mine hired to replace me told me about it! It is a little over a year old! He has only been to it once! He said they sit around campfires and talk about saving our earth! About planting trees. Getting the beavers back on our streams and what we can do to save our earth! It sounds like a party to me! I want to see once! I'm not saying I'm going to join! Just look! It's at the old Jones place. You know Bill, all that's left is that big old barn."

"Yeah, I know. I rode my mule past it the other day. Somebody put a new tin roof on it! They had left the gate open, the cows were in there, it looked like they were eating newly planted trees! I rode in and chased the cows out! As soon as I got them through the gate, they split up, some went up the road and some went down! When I stopped chasing the up bunch, the down bunch were almost to the gate! I drove my mule as fast as it would go to beat them! When I looked back, the up bunch were all headed back down the road! Well, I had to close the gate! It is one of the drop post wire ones. What a pain in the ass one of those are if you can't get off your horse! I use a strap, you know with the hook. I snagged the bottom wire and dragged the post to where I wanted it. Well, anyway, I got it done!"

Eric said, "I want to know how you did the rest?"

Bill looked at faces and decided they all wanted to know! "Well, I am glad I started taking that old cane with me. I used it to get the wire loop over the bottom of the post! Then I hooked the top wire with the strap! This may sound easy but by this time I was tuckered out and all the cows were back to see if they would be able to open the gate when I left! I had to turn the mule around, hook the top wire again and back up! Then, I used the strap around the gate post to draw it close enough to put the top hoop on! When you have time, Tom, I need to go see Slinky again! I want him to make a seat belt to hold my ass in the saddle. I almost fell out of it once. I don't know if I could get back on by myself or not!"

Kate said, "It sounds like it could be a pretty shifty meeting. I don't think I'll go! You guys go. I may go next time if you have fun!"

Friday, Bill rode his mule over. Tom would haul him back!

Eric said in the truck on the way over. "Who are these people?"

"I don't really know, but we will find out!"

Notes? Questions? Ask. I know. No T.V. no games, no computer! I think. I understand. I know! Ask Eric the blue Sage!

At the Jones place there were already 200 cars, vans, trucks and one school bus! They had to park way up the road! Bill gave Eric and Tom a ride down! Tony, Archie, and Nikki were greeting people at the gate! Nikki said, "Welcome. Drive careful! There are a lot of people here! We like to see new faces! We, one of us, will talk to you later! Hi Rohn, you're late, where you been?"

"I had a flat and no jack. Can you believe that?"

Tom, Eric, and Bill were out of hearing range to know what they were saying now! Eric said, "Did you see Rohn? He is the biggest man I have ever seen!"

"Yeah!" Bill said. "He's not anyone to toy with!"

Tom said, "I have seen him and talked to him before! He boxed in the Army. He was the heavy weight champ! But he is a nice guy! If I get the chance I will introduce you!"

Someone was starting a fire already! Hell, it was still in the eighties. They went over to see who. It was Miron. Bill and Tom both knew him. They had both worked with him for a short time in the packing house! They asked him about his ranch! He told them he had turned into a tree hugger. It was hard for Bill and Tom to believe! Miron told his story. He told how hard it had been to keep the cows watered and fed the last few years! He told them about Nikki's and Archie's ranch, T.P. of T.P., Tony and the base. He talked a long time!

Someone was yelling at them, "Food!"

Eric said, "Let's go!" He understood what Miron was saying about the ranch. He had, back in Chicago, watched the world's weather a lot! He knew the southwest was getting hotter and drier! He understood why! What he could not understand was why it wasn't being talked about on the news, what we the people could do stop it! To help to slow it; to make it better! Why not plant more trees? Why not cut back? Why not slow down and think? What is wrong with us? We can save our earth!

WOW! A whole cow being cooked at one time! Eric had never seen anything like this before! Three, three whole cows being cooked. They had labels: fat, mean and lean! Eric asked Miron which one he should eat.

Mixon said, "All three sounds OK to me!"

Eric headed for the chow line. Miron asked Bill, "How are you getting along without your legs?"

He said, "If I tell you the story you have to promise you won't tell!"

"Okay"

Miron said, "Shoot!"

"Well, I lost my wife the same day I lost my legs! It was very hard the first years! I was going to kill myself three or four times! Then his mom sent Eric to me! I quit drinking, got the place cleaned up and started eating better! Eric is a very smart boy! I am learning a lot from him!"

"When he asked me which one he should eat I knew! You can tell I got one like him! She is here tonight. If it wasn't for me, the way I am, she would have hugged me at the gate! I don't like goodbyes, church, public scenes! She winked she understands. She started telling me to sell beef when the price was high, before she was ten! I wish I would have been smart enough to listen. I would have a place like Archie's and Nikki's by now! Have you heard about their place?"

"Not much. It's green, it's cool, and it's wonderful!" It was a lady yelling earlier!

"She's got it right! It is beautiful! You have to see it to believe it! So much wildlife! Birds, reptiles, amphibians, animals. He has moose! Three: a bull, a cow and a calf! He has the state record mule deer on his place this year! The bids are up to $30,000—can you believe that, for a deer? I used to shoot them for fun! It's what my dad told me to do!"

"He charges $10 an hour to fish on his place and he won't tell you what to use! Barbless hooks only. Shit, I do wish I could go back and change things sometimes! My place would be nice!"

"Yeah!" Bill said. "I know! It took me 10 seconds to lose my legs and over sixty years to understand it is us, we are the controllers, the herders, the teachers, the doers, the buyers, sellers, the animal that is killing our earth!?

"You're right!" Miron said. "This last year I have had the biggest loss I have ever had!"

Eric said, "Sell all but your house and yard to the church. That way you can be caretaker and not have any cows to worry about! How does that sound?"

"Good! How come you're so smart about this so fast?" asked Bill.

"Well, I was talking to an old guy in the chow line. He said that's what the church is doing, buying up the ranches cheap and keeping the owners on as caretakers! They keep the hands when they can too! It sounds like a good plan to me! I'll ask Tony about it! He will know!"

"I wonder why, well, I haven't heard? But, I know I haven't been out and about much; I haven't said my place is for sale! I don't go like I used to, I can't afford the gas! I'm going to find Toots, Tony, Archie, and Nikki. Someone to talk to about it, if I can get out of the hole and keep my place I will do it! See you later!"

Eric said, I'm going back for more food. Want to go?"

Tom and Bill asked at the same time, "Which beef did you have?"

Eric said, "All three! I like the mean one best! But they are all good! If you try the great big bowl of potato salad. Don't get very much it's not very good!"

If Eric didn't like any kind of food, it was bad! They did not try to keep up with Eric in the chow line. He got what looked like a leg of beef, then left!

Later, on the way back to the ranch, Bill asked Eric about the leg of beef! Eric said he cleaned it off pretty good then took what was left out to the coyote pups outside of camp. He said he could hear them whining! He thought he smelled them too! Something must have happened to their mom! "Bill, if you would, I would like to have you check on them once in a while!"

"Only if you come with me. I will not do that gate again!"

Tom said, "I have a gate at my place that I am not using. Do you guys want to help me put it up in the morning? I think we might have to put in a new gate post to hold the hinge side!"

Eric asked, "If we use two steel posts and wire the existing post to them, will it work?"

Tom said, "It's worth a try. What do you think, Bill?"

"I think it will work. Let's bring another gate post, just in case!"

Eric said, "Let's make a list of what we will need! I want to make the list, you guys help me if I forget something!"

"Okay" Tom said. "There is a clip board under the seat on your side, Eric!"

Eric said, "Okay. Gate, gate post, four t-posts, hinge pins, wire, shovel, post hole digger, drill, high lift jack, hammer, ½-inch, ¾-inch, and 1-inch wrenches, a digging bar, pliers, post pounder, chain, come-along, and staples! What else?"

"Sounds good. We will sleep on it and add in the morning if needed! I don't know of anything else!"

Bill said, "I want to ride my mule over in the morning!"

The next morning when they got to the Jones' place, Big Rohn was still there! He was fixing fence! Making sure the cows could not get in to eat the trees! He said he had the same plan with the gate! He got his post pounder out of his truck, it was big and heavy, he said he hated the little ones ping, ping, ping.

"Me and my dad made this one when I was a kid about 40 years ago! I'll bet I've put in 10,000 posts over the years. Everybody hired me to use it when I was young! Fifty cents a post I made-damn near $100 in one day once!"

Eric asked Rohn why he was so big. "Was your dad big?"

"No. He was five-feet, ten-inches and about 180 punds, but mom's dad was big—not as big as me, but bigger than most! I think a lot of it is his fault. I used to stay with him when I was growing up! He used to like to watch me eat! He would be cooking breakfast when I woke up in the mornings! It was great! Oatmeal, eggs, steak or bacon, homemade bread! Milk as much as I wanted! Butter. We made that ourselves. It was fun to eat and watch him watch me! He was kind of a tree hugger! He cut back his herd when I was staying with him! He said he was sure most of the ranchers were running too many cattle! We fenced his yard, that's when dad helped me make the post pounder! I told him how bad I hated the little one, ping, ping, ping! I still hate that sound! He, my grandpa, used to plant trees. I wish I wouldn't have, but I sold his place about 15 years ago. It is a pretty place now with no cows and all the trees! I think it was Toots at the café that started grandpa planting trees!"

Eric asked, "Can I try your post pounder?" Rohn got the first post started! He left the post pounder on the post and told Eric to go ahead!

Eric was 14 years old, six-feet, two-inches and in good shape, but he only weighed 150 pounds! He could use it, he drove the first post. He said, "This must weigh 80 to 100 pounds!"

Big Rohn said, "No. We weighed it years ago at the feed store, my friends wanted to, 63 pounds. That's all!" He put in the next post—four hits!

Tom put in the next one, the third post around the hinge gate post! Bill started wiring the posts together! Tom got the brace and bit to drill the hinge pin holes! Eric and Rohn got the gate and one more post out of his truck! They marked where the holes need to be. Tom started drilling. Eric asked if he could drill the next hole. "Sure!" Big Rohn said. He got him started, put in the first hinge pin then let Eric put in the bottom one after he drilled the hole! Eric and Rohn set the gate on the pins! They put the last two posts where they needed to be to latch the gate, wired the tops together and closed the gate!

"Done!" Tom said. "Bill, you try it out. If you can work it anybody can!"

Bill pulled his four wheeler up to the gate, used his cane to unlatch the gate, pushed it open and drove in. He turned around and closed the gate! "Much better!" he said with a smile. "Can we help with something else while we are here, Rohn?"

"Well, yes, if you have time I want to put a block and tackle in the barn, but I don't have a ladder with me! We can kill the beef here for the next meeting if we have some place to hang them! It will be easier!"

"Let's go look!" Bill said. Eric squeezed between the latch post and the fence.

"Smart ass!" big Rohn said as he opened the gate for him and Tom. In the barn they looked at how high the rafters were. Rohn said, "I guess I will have to wait until I get a ladder!"

"No!" Tom and Bill said together.

"Eric can do it!" Eric went to the side of the barn and climbed up! He was standing on the bottom board of the center rafter in 30 seconds. "Is this where you want it?"

Bill said, "I will get the rope and the block and tackle. Get that short chain too. They are all in the back of my truck!" When he got back he had all they needed! Rohn threw the rope over the rafter and hooked the chain on it. Eric pulled the chain up and hooked it around the rafter. They pulled the block up and hooked it on the chain and came down the ropes on the tackle!

"Anything else?" Eric asked as he came down!

"No." Rohn said. "Let's have lunch! I don't know what? I have some left over beef and a loaf of homemade bread!"

Tom said, "I don't know what Kate my wife fixed for us, but it will be good, it always is!"

"I hope its tuna fish," said Eric.

"Yuck!" Big Rohn said. "I don't like it!"

"You will like hers!" Eric said.

Bill said, "Me and Eric will go get the cooler. Where's your lunch Rohn?"

"It's in the cab of my truck. Just bring the box."

There was a picnic table in one end of the barn. That's where they had lunch when Bill and Eric got back! Rohn had salt and pepper beef, a loaf of homemade bread and butter! Kate had fixed nine tuna fish sandwiches and four peanut butter and raspberry jam. They ate almost all of the food! Rohn said, "This is the only tuna fish sandwich I ever ate that I liked!" He ate two of them.

Eric said, "Let's go check on the pups!"

Rohn said, "What pups?" Eric told him about the pups! Rohn said, "I don't like coyotes!"

Bill said; "The year I lost my legs, when I got home I had an invasion of mice! I don't know why, but there were hundreds of them! I was drinking and not sleeping at night! I was sitting on my porch in my wheelchair, there was a full moon, the coyotes, about five or six of them, came in my yard at two o'clock in the morning! I sat and watched them! They killed mice! It was fun to watch them. One would dig, the others would watch. When a mouse would make a run for it, they would grab him so fast it was hard to see. Two bites then swallow! They came back every night! I started leaving the porch light on and the door to my house open. They did not care. On about the fifth or sixth night a mouse ran into the house. The biggest dog of the pack ran right past me and ate the mouse. After that the house was open to the hunt. After about two weeks, I did not see mice or coyotes anymore! I set a few mouse traps. I think I caught four or five mice in the traps. I still catch one once in a while! But, without the coyotes I could have lost my house! It's hard to believe but true! The only time I saw more mice was at a farm once! They were trapped in a granary with a water leak!"

"So, are you feeding the pups?" Rohn asked.

"Well," said Eric. "I did at church last night! But, that's the first thing I did was feed them! You know you can break the bones and give them the marrow out of them too. That's some of the richest food there is!" Eric shut up. He was thinking, *How the hell did I know that?* It has to be from my uncles. They were all survivors, camping, hunting, shooting, playing outside! They were always talking, explaining why they thought like they did!"

"Food!" said Bill. "See, just like my old dog! As soon as you say 'food' he snaps to attention!"

"You were telling us about bone marrow. How do you know what you know?"

"Two places, my uncle's and the old Indian I met and talked to! Both of them said it was very nourishing food! When I think about it I can see they are right! It would be very rich!"

"Let's go break bones and feed the coyotes!" Big Rohn said. "I heard you chased the cows out of here and closed the gate Bill. Thanks!"

"You're welcome"

All the bones from church were in a wash. They were picked clean. There were rocks in the bottom of the wash! So, they climbed down and started breaking bones. Big Rohn said; "This reminds me of fighting in the Army. I had an upper cut from hell! They, the other boxers decided to not fight me! All of the fights were crooked after that! The fighter would come to me and tell me how to throw the punch, and then they would lay down, fight over! It was okay. I had broken enough bones! My first five fights, all my opponents had broken bones! That's why all the fights were fixed!"

Eric asked, "Could you have quit if you wanted?"

"Yes, but if I did I would go to the front lines! I was too big and slow. I would have died! This looks like a lot more than three or four pups! This looks like three or four packs!"

Eric asked Rohn why he said that, how he could tell? Rohn said, "Look at the tracks, that's more coyote tracks than I have ever seen in one place before!"

"You know," said Tom.

"My dad said once that coyotes eat whatever there are too many of. It's like Bill's mice or the grasshoppers one year when I was a kid. There were millions of them. We always had grasshoppers on the farm. But nobody had ever seen them like this before! We burned them. They closed the schools for two weeks! We made a trap that hooked on the front of the truck. It scooped the hoppers up and funneled them under the front tires of the truck. It worked, but there were too many! After a week or two the birds came, lots of them, all kinds. My aunt had told everybody to stop feeding the cats and dogs! Let them eat hoppers! Anyway, that's when the coyotes came. Lots of them. We made a rule at church and school, do not shoot the coyote! They are eating the grasshoppers. We did not get any peas out of our gardens that year, but we did get some crops later! It was quite an experience! I can still remember seeing the coyote droppings on the roads! Little rolls of hopper legs!"

"Does your back ever bother you, Rohn?" Eric asked.

"Yeah! Sometimes all I do is use crutches at home and exercise! I do push-ups. I do curls, I do others at times, but the crutches work to relieve low back pain. For me, anyway!"

Bill said, "Boy, I wish I would have known that years ago before I had back surgery!"

"Yeah!" Big Rohn said. "I had it too!"

Eric asked, "What do they do? Back surgery?"

Bill said, "It can be anything from a discectomy to nerve work! The point is to use crutches. They relieve the pressure and help it heal!"

"Did the surgery help?" asked Eric.

"Well," Bill said. "At the time I told myself it did! But, in the long run, if I would have known and got on crutches instead, I would have been better off! Back surgery was BAD! It changed me! I have never been the same! Most likely I never will!

Tom said, "I was going to have it once. My old doc told me not to. He told me to start hanging around whenever I could, you know, like pull-ups! He told me to get my stomach muscles in the best shape they had ever been in. It worked! He wanted me to do sit-ups too, but I never have been able to do them. I can remember my last year in school. I had to do 100 of them to get an "A" in gym! The eigth grade! It was the only class I could get an "A" in so I did it but it hurt like hell! My right leg is 1-inch shorter than my left. I broke my upper leg bone two times at seven and eight-years-old! I think that's the cause of my back pain when I have it!"

Bill asked, "When is the next meeting?"

Rohn said, "We have them every Friday and Saturday! Time is when you want to show up! This one was the biggest yet, about eleven hundred people showed up! The church is growing. There are a lot of people that want to help save our earth! We, the church, are going to split up into smaller meetings places. They, Nikki and Archie, have papers now so they can marry people. They have had six weddings already! They have them at their ranch!"

Bill said, "We had better be getting home. Thanks!"

"Thanks to you guys! Will we see you at the next meeting?"

"Yes!" said Tom. "I will bring Kate and Joe!"

At the next meeting, Eric was not with them! He had been missing for five days! Bill had told the Sheriff on the fourth day!

Tony, Nikki, Archie, and a lot of people were up here at the gate. They were all under umbrellas, standing close! Nikki came over and gave her dad a hug when he came in. She whispered, "I know you don't like it, but I love you. I'm glad you have become an understander!"

He said, "Me too!"

When Bill showed up, he had a beach umbrella on his mule. It was big. He said, "I don't like being wet! I rode over in the truck with Kate,

Tom, and Joe. They all helped me rig it when we got here! I knew the storm was coming, so I dug this out of the garage! You know you don't realize how much you depend on people until they aren't there! I sure do miss Eric! I hope the little prick is okay. I call him that because I love him! He is like having a thorn—a prick in your side that feels good when you scratch it! I sure hope he is alright!"

The Sheriff showed up about sundown and said he wanted to talk to Bill, no one else.

CHAPTER FIVE

It was dark before they found Bill! Later, Bill found out there were over 2,000 people there. For some reason their cell phones did not work at the Jones' ranch!

The sheriff said, "I talked to Sneeky. He is an Indian! He knows who goes where and what they do! He had seen Eric with the old Indian woman in the west fork! They had built a house. It was like the old Indian's, facing south for the heat of the Sun in the winter. He would not tell me where, but Eric is okay. I wanted to talk to you first because I want you to know about a belief of mine! I believe we have people come around every 100 years or so that are knowers, seers! I think Eric is one of them! You do what you can to take good care of that boy!"

Bill went over to tell Tom, Joe, Nikki, Miron Big Rohn, Archie, and the others around the fire that Eric is okay! "He is back with the old Indian woman in the hills. I think he learns a lot from her. When we used to talk, when he first got here, he would interrupt! But, after he stayed with her he wouldn't! He would listen and think before he would talk! He is a very smart boy! I wonder how smart sometimes."

Kate said, "I am damn near 60 and every time he comes in to help me in the kitchen with lunch or dinner, whatever, I learn from him! He thinks! He understands! He knows!"

"Thank you guys! I know I am learning! I know you are helping! I know you care and so do I! I am sorry for worrying you! But I have to go with the flow sometimes! I can't stop! It is how I am!"

"It's okay, Eric," said Bill. "When you can let us know where you are and what you are doing, please do! We worry. We know you are with your 90-year-old girlfriend having a good time! It's okay, but let us know!"

Eric said, "It is like a different time zone when I am with her! I think about what the west was like 800 years ago, before whites! You know, before US! Before white! B.W.! It was better! I have learned to think and I do! I have a hard time going to sleep at night without thoughts of her and thoughts of hers! She is like an answering machine but better! She tells you what mood the caller is in! What they want! We think and talk. One may not say something for an hour. It's okay to think! Think! Think! Then talk understanding! It takes time and timing!"

"I know!"

Eric said, "I am starting to understand! It will take time for all of us! Think, it is us, we the people! We can control what is happening to our earth! Think! I used to play computer games in Chicago. I would run down hallways and shoot people! Then one day I thought! What if Uncle Frank understood! He told me that back in the 80s electronics are getting 10 times smaller each year! What is possible! He heard back in the 60s. The only thing that keeps "them" from having cybots, robots, was balance. The Segway took care of that!"

In the last few years I have run into people that are not all there! Cybots? Maybe? How much are we the people cybots? Let's see: we are programmed to do what we do! School, work, church, peers, and more! We behave the way they want us to behave because of our programming! <u>Think</u>!

We buy what we don't need! We kill the green! We kill the dandelion! Why?

You are programmed to! Think! The dandelions are fun to play with! Good to eat! They hold the soil in place! Why would we want to kill them? <u>Programming</u>! <u>Think</u>! Yes, it is us in control! We the people! The World is watching; what are we going to do to save our earth?

The beaver is working! He is working for free! I have not seen a bill yet! Think! Save our earth! It is us in control!

"Food!" said Bill. "See, I told you it would work! The lines are forming—lots of them!" Eric asked Kate what she had brought and where is it? She said, "Potato salad. It's in my big red bowl. I don't have any idea where it is!"

Rohn said, "I saw a big red bowl on the end of the third table over there!" He pointed!

Eric was gone. He had not had much to eat in the last few days. Staying with the Indian was fun and a good learning experience, but they did not eat enough to keep Eric going. She had told him how to get to the Jones' place. She said, "I used to go there sometimes to visit with the Jones before the flood washed them out!" He had run most of the way! He did not know how far it was, but it was a long way. He would ask later!

He loaded his plate with beef and Kate's potato salad. He started back to the fire, everyone was gone! He sat down to eat. Lucky came out of the dark and sat down by his feet and watched him eat! He would wait until Nikki or Archie came back before he fed him anything. Archie came back with a bone for Lucky! Lucky went back into the darkness with his bone. Eric asked Archie how he was doing.

Archie said, "Damn near perfect! I am feeling better than I have for years!" He started talking about the ranch, swimming, walking, working, writing, and how much better he felt since he had left the base! How good his life was and how much better it is now! "I am loving it!" He asked Eric about his!

Eric said, "I will tell you all about it when I get back with more food!" He came back with a rib bone for Lucky and full plate for himself.

Nikki followed. He sat down and started eating. Miron, Rohn, Tony, Toots, Dustin, and lots of people Eric did not know came out of the darkness with chairs and food! Dustin said, "We want to know about living with the Indian, Eric?"

"Well, I thought about that on my way over here! I knew someone would ask. I think the best way to tell would be to imagine being able to talk to your great grandma! Someone who will not lie to you. Who knows what life was like before we the white man got here. Someone who understands that it is us; we are the disease that's killing our earth! I learn all kinds of things from her. What to eat, what not to eat, how to tan leather, how to be patient, and how to use our earth! How to use a small fire, how to live with what you have! How to survive. I kind of miss you guys when I am out there, but most of all I miss the food! I'm going back for more. I won't be long!" He left for the chow lines!

Archie asked Bill, "Where did he come from?"

Bill said, "Chicago, but that's not what you want. Is it?"

Archie said, "Well, yes and no! How can a kid come from Chicago and be living with an old Indian in the hills and liking it? That's what I want to know!"

Bill said, "He is very smart. He learns very fast! I think I am learning more from him than he is learning from me! When the Sheriff told me where he was, he said Eric is very special, take good care of him! I think he will impress all of us in time! I think I will ask him to only stay two or three days at a time with his friend! That way he won't get so hungry!"

Rohn said, "He eats like I did when I was a kid! Nobody could understand where it all went! This is his third trip to the chow line right?"

Lucky came into the fire light, got another bone and then left!

Eric came back. His plate did not have very much food on it! Bill asked if he was alright. He said, "I think I have had enough for tonight. I want to lay down and rest."

Dustin said, "I keep an old sleeping bag in the back of my truck in the tool box. You can use that if you want."

Bill said, "How did you get here tonight?"

Eric said, "I ran, then walked when I got tired!"

"From West Fork?"

"Yes."

"That's 30 miles! You should rest!"

"Good Night." Eric asked Dustin which truck was his.

"The red one with the bulging bed behind the cab. It's close to the gate. I got here early"

Eric went to bed!

The group around the fire started talking about smaller meetings. This was the biggest one so far! It was too big. There were too many people and not enough parking!

"How do you fix it?" Dustin asked.

Nikki said, "Multiple meeting sites! Go to the one closet to home! It won't be hard!'

"We need a letter," Archie said. "Tony said it's in the works! We should have it by next weekend. We can list the meeting sites in it and give the good news!"

"How big is it?"

"Two pages. I will copy it on my copier and mail them, but the church will have to help with postage and paper. We think we have about 1200 names on the mailing list."

Archie said, "That won't be a problem. That is, we the people of the church have put a lot of money in the…"

BANG! BANG!

Gun shots? "Sheriff, what the hell's going on?"

Someone said, "Somebody took the money box off the gate post. Cowboy Bud got two shots off at the tires. He thinks he got 'em! We are going up the road after them! Wait for me!"

The sheriff yelled, "I don't want one of those kids shooting some-body, unless I'm there!"

Eric ran up the road to where the two girls had ran off the road! He opened the door. They were both crying. "Please help us. We don't want to go to jail!"

Eric said, "Follow the water up that way. Wait under the bridge and I will be back in the morning!" He picked up the cash box out of the truck bed and packed it to the road. The sheriff's truck came up the road. Eric put the cash box in the back!

He pointed, "The truck is right there; nobody in it!"

Eric walked back to the camp fire. He said, "I have something to talk about but we have to talk before we do anything! Okay?" He looked at faces around the fire, thirteen people. He told them the story. "What do you think we should do?"

Tony said, "Give them to the sheriff. Let him handle it!"

Dustin asked, "How old are they?"

Eric said, "They didn't seem very old! The truck cab light did not come on. It was too dark to see faces, maybe 16, I would guess!"

Archie asked, "Were they really scared, or putting on a show?"

"They were really scared. I could feel it coming off them! It was strange!"

"It is strange. I could smell it sometimes coming off my men in Vietnam! I wonder if they would fit in at Matt's place? He's a friend that handles bad, good girls!"

"That would be best for the girls," Nikki said.

"Let's pick them up in the morning, take them to Tom's place and see what kind of people they are, then decide! I'm going back to bed," Eric said. He headed for the truck.

Archie said, "That's where I should be going too!"

Tony said, "I did not hear or see anything. I'm going home!"

Nikki said, "Can we go with you to pick up the girls. I want to listen and ask questions when they talk? Is that okay, Archie?"

"Yes!" He said. "An adventure will be good for us; we can sleep in the truck. We have food. Nikki, why don't you make the rounds at the food tables and get us lunch for tomorrow, maybe more!" She got up and left. Archie yelled, "There is ice in the cooler!"

She said, "Okay!"

Archie said, "I did not want to say it when she was here, but she will be a very good person to have at the trial. We will be judge and jury, playing God! I think we can do a better job than our court systems today!"

"What's that?" The Sheriff said.

"I was just saying that from what I understand, our justice systems really are bad nowadays. Sending people to prison that should not be there! And letting the bad guys go if he has enough money! Did you find him?"

"No," The sheriff said. "The truck was reported stolen three weeks ago by a farmer that said it could have been three months ago. He said he doesn't use it in the spring. It gets stuck too much. Two-wheel drive! He said the keys were in it! Anybody could have taken it. There was nothing in it!"

Cowboy Bud said, "I was looking at the tires, not the driver!"

"No one else saw them as far as we know!"

"You said 'them". Dustin said. "How do you know" "Well it's easy. There were two ass marks in the seat, no dust on the seat where they were!" "I want to know how much money was in the cash box so I know how to charge them. I am going back out looking for them tonight, so if you can, count it for me."

"Lights would help." Nikki said.

The sheriff brought his truck over. "You can count it inside if you want!"

"No. Many hands make light work. I hate idling trucks, but we will count it. Have you got a clip board and paper?"

"Yes."

"Got it!" They started counting and totaling. $27,000 was what they came up with! It would be recounted later, before deposit!

"Sheriff, that's enough for grand theft!"

"I'm going hunting! I will fry their asses stealing from the church!"

The aheriff left with Bud and a few of the other cowboys!

"What time is it?" asked Archie.

"5 A.M." said Dustin. "It gets light at 6 a.m….Has someone got coffee?" He asked.

"Yeah! It's on," Dustin said. "Let's have breakfast and go to Tom's and Kate's. Does that sound okay? I have about four dozen eggs. What is left from last night?"

Nikki said, "A lot of food, bread, and salads. Someone start making cowboy toast!"

Big Rohn said, "I have side of pork, beef, eggs, and maple syrup." Faces came out of the dark! People nobody knew! "We are here to help! We have orange juice! Hot cake fixings, cranberries. If you have not had cranberry on pancakes, you haven't lived! I am Jay, I understand! I know you are trying to save our earth. We are too! There are about 100 of us here tonight! We have been watching you. We want in. We want to help save our earth!"

Archie asked, "Where did you come from?"

"We," Jay said, "are from all over the U.S.A. We even have one from China! Trust us. We want to save our earth!"

Well, it was a very good breakfast! A lot of telephone numbers and addresses changed hands! At 6:30 four trucks headed for Tom's at the bridge. Tom stopped the truck! "Okay," Eric yelled. "Come on!" The girls came running. Eric said, "Get in the bed of the truck. Cover up! The sheriff is looking for you! If we stop to talk to him—don't move!"

Under the sleeping bag the girls found water, bacon, hot cakes, and oranges. They ate and talked!

"How do you want to play it?"

"Well, we have found a gold mine! If we play it right we can be free!" They were sisters. They had come to the U.S. to be free! Not to be thieves or sex slaves, but they were! They had seen each other in the mall, and left running! Running, hiding, not knowing where they were going!

They passed the sheriff and waved. No problem. Archie kept telling Nikki to drive faster. She said, "No. I want this to last! It is an adventure! Haste makes waste!"

Well, at Tom's house the girls took the spare bedroom. Tom's dogs would tell everybody if they try to sneak off. Everybody went to sleep! It was noon when Nikki woke up! Archie was fondling her in his sleep! She laid there and enjoyed it! What a dream! She could hear the creek; she could hear someone else moving around. They had parked the truck right next to the kitchen window. She pushed Archie away and got up.

When she went in the house it was just like when her mom, well just like home! Kate was baking bread! Mixing the second batch!

"Do you want coffee?" Kate asked when she came in.

"Water first, then coffee. Where are the cups?"

"On the right side of the sink!"

"How do you think we should handle the girls?" Nikki asked.

"Just tell them that if they lie to us we will call the sheriff. Then, have them tell their story! Let them talk if they will."

Archie came in and said, "Bill and Eric are at the gate. I heard them pull up! I think they want to be sure we are up before they come in!" Nikki gave Archie a cup of coffee. "I will go out and wave them in." She said. "Bill parked by the kitchen door." He had forgotten his other wheelchair. They all knew he liked his mule better. Joe came through the gate and parked under the elm tree next to Big Rohn's truck! Dustin was coming around the shed! Kate came out with coffee and cups for them. She said, "We will use the shed, the house is not big enough."

Tom came out of the house with raspberry jam, butter, and hot bread. He pulled the top off a loaf and said, "Help yourselves. I'm not going to wait on you! Eric, give me a hand with the picnic table." They moved it into the shed! Eric went with Tom to get chairs! They set the chairs up in a circle! Kate went in the house to get the girls! Nikki told everybody what the plan was.

Rohn said, "It sounds good! K.I.S.S. Keep It Simple Stupid."

Kate came out with the girls, gave them coffee and said, "We will decide what to do with you! If you lie to us we will give you to the sheriff. This is Rohn, Tom, Eric, Dustin, Archie, Bill, Nikki, Joe, and I'm Kate. Tell us your story."

"We, I'm Connie. This is Pat, my sister. We decided last night we will tell the truth! No lies, but we will leave some of the names and places out of our story until we get to know you better! We come from a small farm in another country. The farm was drying up, dying! Our aunt lives in Boston. She took us in and helped us come over! We did not know, but she is a bad person. She had us stealing from stores. She made Pat go live with a man she did not know! She would take me shopping. I would cause a scene and she would steal things! I would leave after she did! I saw Pat in the mall one day and we ran. We did not know where we were or where we were going, we just ran! We asked a man and his wife for a ride at as gas station. They had Utah plates on their car. They said they were going to turn us in at the next town when we were pretending to be asleep! We ran when they stopped for gas. That's when we found the truck! Keys were in it! We have been stealing gas, begging for money and food, driving back roads and sleeping in the truck. I was driving. Pat saw someone put money in the box on the gate! We were scared and hungry! You know the rest!"

The circle decided they did not want to hear anymore. Archie called Matt and told him the story! He said; "Yes, I will take them! Can you bring them?" Archie said; "I will call you back!" "You know, we could get in trouble for this!" Nikki said; "We can fix a hideout in the back of the truck for them, but we need to tell the girls about the school first and make sure it is what they want!" They did and the girls said yes!

Archie said, "We can go to the ranch today and drive on down in the morning!" The guys went out to fix Archie's truck! Archie called Matt back and said, "We will see you tomorrow!"

Tom had a tarp for the cover, ropes and bungees. The bedding was already there. They used 2 x 4s across the bed of the truck, with a 4-foot x 8-foot sheet of plywood! The tarp on top! A lot of ropes and bungees to keep the tarp from flapping! The tailgate was the door to the house! It looked like a load of plywood covered and tied down!

Rohn said, "I will be going. Good luck. See you all later!" Joe, Bill and Eric left too. The girls had gone in the house to take showers. Kate had gone with them to help and to find something for the girls to wear. Dustin had gone for a walk! The girls were ready and almost in the truck when Dustin came back with a shirt full of raspberries. He gave some to all and said goodbye!

On the road, Nikki said, "Will you drive. I want to write? Yes to the oil!"

"Okay" They made it back to the ranch late in the day! Connie and Pat loved the place and asked why is it so pretty?

"Can we go for a walk?"

Archie said, "You girls go for a walk and I will fix dinner!" The moose was laying down on the other side of the beaver pond! The girls had never seen one, or a beaver.

When Nikki told them about taking the cows off the range, Connie said, "We have goats at home! They eat everything and anything! We had to hang our clothes up, way up, or the goats would eat them! You know they are the reason our farms are dying at home. Everyone has goats! The goats even climbed trees and ate the leaves! The owners are too dumb to see!"

Pam said, "And they pray for rain, too dumb to see the rains wash the top soil away! Pray for fewer grazers! That might work! But they are too dumb to see it is us! We are the disease that is killing our trees, raising our seas, increasing our breeze, freezing our peas, killing our earth! Get the beaver back!"

"Okay. That's it! I want you to say that to Archie! I want to go back to the house"

Pam said, "Can I look at their dam before we go?"

"Okay, but only for a minute!" She walked down the stream, then crossed the stream. She was looking at the dam as she walked. She was, as they say, taking it all in! She walked across the upper end of the pond up to her hips, and then went back. She did not want to make the fish stink, is what she said later! When she got through, she walked back to the house without saying a word!

Inside, Archie was frying eggs! Lots of them! Three dozen. Why? That's all there was: eggs! "What are you doing? What are you doing with all those eggs? Are you cooking and thinking?"

"Yes. I was thinking the girls could use a good protein fix! I could tell by the way the truck bed smelled! They have had a lot of greens, maybe grass! I can't explain, but I could tell! They can use a good protein fix! Please don't yell at me. I don't like it! Private!"

"Okay," Nikki said. "I will do my best, Sir!"

"You know I don't like that either, Private."

"Stop calling me that, Sir!"

"Okay, Nik. Will you set the table?'

"Yes, I will ,Arch!"

Pam asked if they had a pencil and paper she could use. Archie said, "I know she is an artist! Give her my art supplies." Nikki had started setting the table. The girls were finishing! She went and got the art supplies. Pam started crying and drawing. She was in a hurry to get started! She made an outline of the pond! She started shading the banks! She shaded the dam, the water, the rocks, the trees: It was like painting by numbers. She was good! "Okay," said Archie. "Let's eat!" Connie got a plate full of eggs and started feeding her sister, by hand, no fork!

Archie and Nikki started eating and watching the sisters. "Maybe we should rest a day before we take the sisters back," said Nikki.

Archie said, "I was thinking the same thing!"

"She gets like this. I have been feeding her like this for years. All she needs is a paper and a pencil. That's why she started crying.She has never had something like this!"

She was pointing at their world! The house, the pond, the trees, the flowers, the colored pencils, the eggs, the birds, the moose, everything. She was in some kind of shock! Pat did not stop; the sketch was getting better by the minute!

Archie showed Connie how to turn the Coleman lantern off! She said, "We have the same one at home!"

The next morning when Archie and Nikki got up. Pam was still at it! The painting was as good as the real thing, maybe better! It was 'a good life for one and all!'

"How much?" He said. "I like it!"

"$500," Pam said.

"I'll give you $100 and you will be happy!" He said.

"Sold!" Pam said, looking at her sister and smiling. "Okay, yes, they are good people, just like us!"

Archie said, "You know, I would have paid the $500!"

"Yeah! And you know we would have given it to you!"

"Yes!"

"Thanks!"

Nikki said, "I'm going to call Matt!"

Archie said, "Wait until she has finished the painting! I think as long as it doesn't have paint on it, it is a drawing! But, if it does have paint on it, it is a painting! I have decided to have her sign it in paint! Think! There are a lot of people who still can, I hope!"

Think! There are a lot of US, we can save our earth. We can cut back! We can get the beaver back to hold our water on our earth to cool it! Think! If you still can! What happens if you start thinking and stop watching T.V., start understanding, stop playing computer games. Do you become smarter? <u>Yes</u>!

Please think! Eric the Blue Sage!

It is US, we the people who are in control! The rulers!

The girls were asleep when they got to Matt's place. Nikki could not wake them up! She yelled! Shook their feet! Pulled on them; they slept!

She went in the house, big house! She said, "I could not wake them up!"

Archie said, "Battle fatigue. What do you think, Matt?"

"Yeah, a lot of them get it when they get here!"

Nikki said, "How could you, how could anyone sleep that hard?"

Matt said, "A lot of the girls do it! It may be the first night or the 30th day they sleep, sometimes for 24 hours! They knew you and Archie would not hurt them. They knew you were taking them to a safe place. They knew they needed the sleep! They knew the truck was stopping and going. They knew the roads at times, where rough! They knew if the truck stopped for a long time. It's time to get up! They will be in in a minute, you watch! Do you want some soup? It is hot!"

"Is that what you and Ann were having for dinner?"

"Yes! But it is hot. We have a great big pot of it in the fridge! That's the way we cook! We know we may have close to twenty people here without warning! The girls try different recipes! Sometimes they cannot eat them so they come here! We have a lot of food! I have a walk in freezer, a cooler to age beef! Ann is a good cook! If you want something, just ask!"

Nikki said, "I will have the special!"

Archie said, "Me too!"

"I have a lot of guest rooms when the kin come to visit. Who knows how many or what they want? I think you two are sleeping together, so if it's okay you can use number one right next to our house!

"Sounds good to me," said Nikki.

Ann put more soup on to get hot and set the table for four more people! The girls knocked on the door. When they came in they could not stop looking at the animals! Matt had been a big game hunter for years before he lost his sight!

Pat asked Connie if she would get her pencils and paper. Connie said, "After we eat, it looks like soup! I am not going to spend all night spoon feeding you!"

Pat said, "Okay!" But could not stop looking at the animals, bear, cats, a moose, rhinoceros, ugly pigs and lots of horned animals. She had never even seen a picture of a lot of the animals, birds, dogs, etc.

"WOW!" she said. "Where did they all come from?"

Matt said, "All over the World. I will tell you after we eat if you want."

"I want!" said Pat.

"Soup is on." Ann said, "This has a lot of things in it from your ranch Archie. The girls and I made it last night. I would like it if you would tell me what you recognize. Okay?"

"Okay!" said Nikki. "I went picking with them, so I know a lot of them! I will let others go first. This should be fun!"

Pat said, "Wild celery."

"One," said Ann.

"I will count as you name them,"

Connie said, "Mushrooms."

"Yes," said Ann. "About seven; there are a lot of them growing around the beaver ponds. That's two!"

"Raspberry," said Archie.

"Yes. Number three."

"Tumbleweed," said Archie.

"Yes. Number four."

"Pine nuts," said Nikki.

"Yes! Number five."

"Cattails," said Nikki.

"Yes. Number six."

"Grass."

"Yes, at least four of them. That's seven!"

"Blue sage?" asked Pat.

"Yes. Very little, but it is in there. That's number eight."

"Beef?" asked Archie.

"No," said Ann.

It slowed down now! They were tasting, smelling, looking, eating and enjoying!

"Beaver," said Archie.

"No! We would not do that unless we were starving!"

"Rock chuck?"

"No!"

"Rabbit?"

"No!" Archie knew there was some kind of meat. "Porky pine!" Like he knew he had it! "No!" said Ann.

"It's not snake, what the hell is it?" He was thinking how could it be anything else! He would name all the mammals he knew! That would work!

With Matt's hunting and what's available in the southwest, the list was almost endless! Maybe he should try another way! Yes! "Is the meat off my ranch?"

"No!" said Ann.

"Is it from Africa?"

"No!"

"Is it from the southwest?"

"Yes!" Archie was thinking it would not have been goat, sheep or deer. "Is it a mammal?"

"Yes!" "Everyone was watching and listening!

"How about your ranch?"

"Yes!" Ann almost looked like she had a tear in her eye!

"It was their dog or cat!" He would play on this one. This will be interesting! "Was it a hoofed mammal?"

"No!"

"Was it a land mammal?"

"Yes!"

"Was it a rodent?"

"Yes!"

"A chipmunk?"

"No!"

"You guys can help me. What is it?"

Connie said, "A muskrat." In a low quiet voice. We were eating them before we left!"

"Yes!" said Ann.

"That's number nine. I can get you the recipes if you want. We have one girl, who is a fanatic about writing. She will have a recipe! Give or take a little!"

Archie said, "When I was asking questions I saw a tear in your eye and thought it was your dog! Why did you get the tear in your eye?"

Ann said, "I have been thinking about this for years; when I die, I don't want to be buried or burned! I want to live on. I want to be eaten by other living things. I don't care who! A coyote, a bird, a fly, a tree, a weed. I don't want to be useless! I want to live on and on. I don't think we can do this if we keep killing our earth! We are in control. It is US, we decide to kill the beaver, we decide to cut the trees, and we decide to over-graze. It is US; we, me and Matt are understanders! Like it, or not! I will do my best to save our earth, so I can have eternal life! I was thinking about having my dog for dinner! How wonderful for him to live on through me! Or me through him! I hope you can still talk to me?"

CHAPTER SIX

Side Tracked!

This is what I think! I can think! Believe what I want! It is a free country! I have the right to free speech!

We the people are taught, learn, schooled, and programmed to behave the way we do! Sidetracked! T.V., news, radio, school, electronic games, sports, church, etc. It is all sidetracking! We are not talking about what is really important: saving our earth! Our planet! We can control! We can plant more; we can get the beaver back all over our earth! We can use less! We can think! We can change! We can burn less, clear less, etc. We can save our earth! But we have to understand that it is us that are killing our earth! We have to look, see, know, and accept it is <u>US</u>! <u>Understand</u>!

Sidetracked! What do you think will happen if we do nothing! God will save us? Bullshit! Our government will take care of us? Bullshit! We the people have to save our earth if we are going to survive! What do we want? I want a greener, milder, nicer climate! What do you want?

What do you think the news is, the games we play, the education we receive, the T.V., the movies, our phones, if not sidetracking? I feel like a programmed rat. If you do what theywant, you get what you want!

Food, toys, sex, drugs, a massage, and more money! If you don't do what they want, you get pain and more pain! Jail and less pay!

We, the two legged talking rats, are doing what they want; we are killing our earth! Why? Who for? Not US!

Please think about it!

Please talk about it!

Please learn to understand!

It is US, we the people!

Thanks for reading. Eric the Blue Sage!

Sidetracked! Church? You don't have to go every day, but you have to think about it every day, live by the rules or go to hell!

Sidetracked! Work? I know I don't really know what I am doing. Putting chemicals in the water, feeding chemicals to the meat, adding chemicals to the food? Spraying chemicals on the plants! If I don't do what they want, I will be out of work! Turning our water ways into toilets that flush shit to the seas or into our drinking water! Think why are we sending our organic matter to the land fill?

Sidetracked! School is programming, learning to do what they want, so you can help kill our earth and think you are doing the right thing, climbing the ladder, making more money!

Think! That's all I ask!

CHAPTER SEVEN

Instructions

1. Wash your coat in the summer and hang it outside to dry! Cold water works!
2. Wash your bedding in the summer and hang it outside to dry! Cold water works!
3. Wash your coveralls in the summer and hang them outside to dry! Cold water works!
4. Wash anything heavy in the summer; hang it outside to dry! Cold water works!
5. Grow whatever you can! Tomatoes, weeds, trees, and bushes. Did I say weeds? Anything is better than bare ground.
6. Have a compost pile. Don't worry too much about what you put in it! It all turns to shit in the long run! <u>Think</u>!
7. Don't send any more to the land fill than you have to! Most of the shit you send to the land fill winds up in your grandkids drinking water sooner or later. Please. . .for them . . .Save our earth! Think!
8. Don't burn anything unless it is to stay warm!

Think about what you are doing and why? Why would anyone want to kill dandelions? They are good to eat, fun to play with! Pretty. They hold the soil in place! What is wrong with us? Programming! Please think! Why do you kill dandelions? Programming! Yes! It is programming. I understand! Can you? I will never kill another dandelion as long as I live. Eric the Blue Sage. I think! Can you?

Why buy a new car, if the one you have works just fine?

Why move, if you like it where you are?

Why buy, unless you have to?

Why do you want more money?

Programming! Yes! Is this a test? Is it? For me, you, us? Think! Can you understand? It is US killing our earth! I understand, can you? Think! Eric the Blue Sage!

Well, I don't know how to stop, how to end this, but I want the reader to know life does not stop! We are fighting a war! We the people can win! We can change! We can keep learning! We have been following the money for hundreds of years! It's not working! Let's work for the other green, the Earth! Help her! Save her! Defend her! Befriend her! Please think! Mend her!

The trailer park could be any city, town, village, hamlet, ranch, etc. Anywhere on our earth, for our grandkids! Yes! More green is the thing! Get the beaver back! Don't be slack! Don't distract! Attack! Yes, do what you can to help save our earth! Plant, grow, reduce the number of grazers, and start with the people. Buy less, slow down, stop the flow of money, power, mind control, education, etc. To the Top!

To the leaders of our government: Think! Money is killing our earth and we the people are the buyers, ants, two-legged rats, grazers, herders, shepherds, bankers, etc., who are doing it! If we burn, bury, kill the green, clean, clear, remove the organic matter from our earth surface, we are killing her!

152

Let's save our earth for our grandkids! Your grandkids will love you for it! Do what you can to save our earth! Think!

"The People"
My Master Plan!

Let the beaver come back on all the water ways all over the world A.S.A.P!

Recycle! Building materials. Cars, keep them running, don't destroy them! Save brick, two by fours, windows! Etc.

Don't buy new unless you have to! Reuse and save if you can! It is our earth!

Use man power if you can. Track hoes to tear down a building is wrong. They destroy them; the things we should reuse to save our earth! Think!

It is US, we the people in control! Please think! We control! We cut! We burn! We clear! We need! Please think aboutwhat we are doing!!

Why? Who for? Not for us! We want our grandkids to survive! We want our earth to live and love on! We want to fix her!

Think! Eric the Blue Sage

Thanks to Miss Marpole, Lisa, Rose, any and all that helped with my book! My understanding, my spelling! Eric the blue Sage

Think Sheets!

Rat control! Here we are in control! Do you know you, we, me, I am in control? Yes, it is us! We buy, we burn, we bury, we kill the green that can save our earth! Think! Please! Eric The blue Sage!

You, me, he, she, we are the disease that is killing our earth! Think!

We are the two-legged, talking rats, the thinking goats, the pigs, that are killing our earth!

We are programmed to do what we do! Why? Kill the dandelions? They are fun to play with, good to eat, they hold the soil in place why kill them? It is programming! Think!

Think Sheet

Traders? Is that what we should be? Yes! Why kill our earth to keep the rich, rich? I say no! It is time for a change! Let's chase the other green! We the people can control! Let's do it! I don't want a new car, I don't want to learn a new phone, a new remote, a new computer language. I call bullshit! My car, my phone, my remote is good enough! Stop already! I want to think! I want to understand! Not memorize! Thanks!

Eric the Blue Sage